Britain, 1919-1970

Britain, 1919–1970

Edited with an Introduction by
John F. Naylor

A NEW YORK TIMES BOOK

Quadrangle Books
CHICAGO

Library of Congress Catalog Card Number: 71-152096

SBN Cloth 8129-0187-8
SBN Paper 8129-6149-8

The publishers are grateful to the contributors herein
for permission to reprint their articles.

Preface

WHAT IS history all about? The eminent historian of Victorian England, G. M. Young, concluded that "the real, central theme of History is not what happened, but what people felt about it when it was happening." In such a perspective—and the student of history will find few as rewarding—the occasional pieces contributed to the *New York Times Magazine* illuminate the ways in which contemporaries viewed the process of historical change in twentieth-century Britain. Close in time to the events described, the contributors sometimes miss the larger design; certainly they do not possess the advantages of hindsight which accrue to historians. Yet their accounts give the student of history a sense of immediacy with the past, a means of involvement which he ignores at his peril.

Any collection of contemporary accounts demands of the editor a selectivity based upon his perception of the major themes of that particular historical period. Modern Britain has witnessed the creation of a more enlightened and humane industrial society: in this volume, emphasis is laid directly upon the triad of domestic history—political, economic, and social. Some may perceive errors of omission, and I of course accept responsibility for those as well as for errors of commission. At the same time, I am grateful to my graduate assistant, Thomas Dillon, for assembling the materials from which I chose these articles.

Contents

2. Years of Heroism, 1939–1951

3. Years of Reappraisal, 1951–1970

Britain, 1919-1970

Introduction

"NO ONE HAS done more to bring about this splendid victory than you." So, in the aftermath of the First World War, wrote Woodrow Wilson's confidant, Colonel House, to the British Prime Minister David Lloyd George. The tribute was well earned, because Lloyd George, the Welsh-born Liberal, had instilled new vigor in the British war effort at a time when the various European military machines were running down, victims of their common policy of attrition. Yet Lloyd George intended to share such a tribute with the people, who had assumed the burdens of war at home as well as in the trenches. He spoke of making Britain "a fit country for heroes to live in": specifically, he declared his government's intention of providing houses for those heroes. Few if any private homes had been built during the war, and in 1918 estimates indicated the need for more than 600,000 new units. In the vanguard of those who looked to the future—to the reconstruction of the British economic and social fabric—and secure in the nation's debt for his wartime efforts, Lloyd George scored what appeared to be a sweeping electoral triumph in the general election of December 1918 (far more so in terms of parliamentary seats than percentage of the vote cast, as is habitually the case in British politics). Yet to gain that success Lloyd George had paid a political price: continued division within the Liberal party.

In peace as in war, Lloyd George and the former Liberal Prime Minister H. H. Asquith, deposed in December 1916, refused to defer to each other. Consequently Lloyd George had to build his parliamentary support around the Conservatives, his partners in the coalition government he headed. Lacking the freedom of maneuver open to a Prime Minister who is at the same time leader of the largest party in the House of Commons, Lloyd George became, in a sense, a Tory hireling. Trapped by the Germanophobia of the times, particularly strong among the predominant Conservative party, he was forced to play a more vindictive role in the peace conference than he likely wished. Nonetheless he exercised a moderating influence upon the terms of the peace treaty. At Versailles he spoke with two voices: while giving every appearance of advocating a harsh peace, he in fact aimed at a conciliatory peace with Germany. His double game earned him considerable criticism from both flanks. John Maynard Keynes, who resigned in despair from the Treasury delegation at Versailles, won instant recognition with his 1919 publication, *The Economic Consequences of the Peace,* in which he warned that the settlement would be disastrous. The burgeoning Labour party, infused in 1918 with a socialist ideology, viewed the British efforts at peacemaking with a skeptical eye. At the same time a considerable portion of Tories was less than pleased with the spoils of victory.

Nor did reconstruction prove a panacea for national ills: economic problems proved stubborn, even unyielding. Such substantial achievements of Lloyd George's postwar administration as housing, a more comprehensive insurance against short-term unemployment, and an Irish settlement were dwarfed by the expectations of 1918. Industrial unrest increased sharply with the decline of economic activity and the falling wages of 1920–1921. The laboring classes turned elsewhere than to Lloyd George's compromised radicalism to secure their ends. The Labour party provided the alternative, and Britain entered into a short-lived but politically confusing period in which three parties competed for power within a system which functioned best with but two. In that struggle the Liberals were severely handicapped by their wartime internal division, which was now superimposed upon the older problem of adapting historic Liberalism to the twentieth century. The Prime Minister, at once co-author and victim of that recent rupture, had no choice but to make himself the indispensable figure, as he had done in 1918. He spent much of 1922 in pursuing an idiosyncratic, adventurist foreign policy. As a result he exposed Britain to the danger of war in the Near East, a course of action which many in the country thought unjustifiable.

For those who were personally at odds with the Prime Minister to begin with, the Near Eastern crisis confirmed their worst suspicions. Stanley Baldwin displayed a very different temperament from Lloyd George's in objecting to the latter's restless energies: "He is a dynamic force, and it is from that very fact that our troubles . . . arise. A dynamic force is a very terrible thing; it may crush you, but it is not necessarily right." Meeting at the Carlton Club, the Conservative MP's withdrew their support of the coalition. Lloyd George, the last Liberal Prime Minister, resigned; Bonar Law and, shortly thereafter, Baldwin himself, succeeded. In 1923 Baldwin committed the error of identifying the Tories with a specific policy, Protection, which caused him to lose his parliamentary majority in the general election. In turning to Labour, the second largest parliamentary party, whose poll had risen steadily since 1918, King George V exhibited none of the fashionable fear that bolshevism would follow in Labour's footsteps. In January 1924 he invited Labour's leader, Ramsay Mac-Donald, to form a government, wryly confiding to his diary: "Today 23 years ago dear Grandmamma died. I wonder what she would have thought of a Labour Government!" Surely Queen Victoria would not have been amused.

Though MacDonald devoted much of his attentions to the international sphere, serving as his own Foreign Secretary, the minority Labour government nevertheless accomplished significant reform in housing. In other respects its performance was desultory. The men of the people, as the Labour ministers viewed themselves, failed to find an answer to the continuing problem of structural unemployment, which then forced idleness upon slightly more than one million Britons. Yet in relieving the fears that Labour was not fit to govern, the first Labour ministry, however unimaginative they otherwise proved, served the movement well. For his part, Ramsay MacDonald sharpened the guidelines which British foreign policy was to follow for the balance of the decade: England's efforts to bring about the reconciliation of France and

Germany, embodied in the compromise on reparations agreed to in the Dawes Plan, led Europe directly into the Locarno era. MacDonald's Conservative successors negotiated the various Locarno pacts, although they refused to incorporate the Soviet Union within the ranks of the conciliated powers. Though the 1924 recognition of the Soviet government was not withdrawn, the Tories broke off diplomatic relations with Russia between 1927 and 1929. Because their attentions centered on western Europe, the Conservatives did not much mourn the absence of either Russia or the United States from the League of Nations. Moreover, MacDonald shared with Austen Chamberlain a reluctance to view the League as anything but an agency for conciliation; nor did many Englishmen dissent from such a view at the decade's end. In 1928, upon the signing of the Kellogg-Briand pact renouncing the use of war as an instrument of national policy, the need for an agency to enforce the peace seemed to have vanished. The First World War had not, or so it appeared, been fought in vain.

Domestically the scene had cleared as well. By 1924 the prewar level of total industrial production had been regained: employment had risen and so, too, had the standard of living. Yet the problem of unemployment persisted, particularly in the older staple industries, such as coal, engineering, and cotton, which once had been the base of England's industrial supremacy. Exports failed to regain the pre-war level, causing contemporaries to reason that British products had once again to be made competitive in the world market. In order for this to come about, however, wages had to yield to the greater national interest. Not surprisingly, trade union leaders, tempered by wartime experiences and strengthened by Labour's rapid political rise, failed to share such an analysis. The conflict came to a head in the country's largest industry, coal mining, which had a long and troubled history of labor relations. Lloyd George had despaired of mediating between the miners and the mine owners, having once remarked that he thought the miners were the stupidest men in Britain, until he had to deal with the owners. As the coal crisis deepened in 1925–1926, both the Baldwin government and the leaders of the Trades Union Congress attempted to play a mediative role; the latter were anxious to restrain the extremist tendencies of the miners' leaders. The government failed to appreciate the TUC strategy; they could not see beyond the spectre of a general strike, which they construed as a political action subversive of the British constitution. Whatever the accuracy of their perception, the Tory government proved resolute in meeting the general strike of 1926 head-on; since the trade union leaders were determined not to raise the barricades, they quickly admitted defeat. The miners, continuing their strike forlornly, were broken after six months. Labour governments or not, the capitalists kept the upper hand.

British capitalism did not, however, regain world pre-eminence: exports did not attain the pre-war level, though the nation's balance of payments was favorable—Britain's "invisible exports" served to ensure prosperity. Aside from unemployment, which in significant measure affected only those permanently unemployed, the economy was healthy. Contemporaries felt no sense of living in a nation in decline. Though the depression of 1929 increased unemployment, nonetheless it affected Britain in contradictory ways. By December 1930 some 2.5 million were unemployed; yet those still employed found their position improved, because real wages had risen as world prices fell, lowering the cost of British imports. Most Englishmen were remote from the abject despair of unemployment.

As the world economic crisis deepened, Great Britain experienced political repercussions. When English bankers were caught short in the central European financial collapse, they insisted—and for more than symbolic reasons—on bolstering international confidence in the pound. Toward that end they urged a balanced budget upon the Labour government, which had assumed office in 1929, again in a minority capacity. Though MacDonald and Philip Snowden, the Chancellor of the Exchequer, placed great stock in the advice of the financial community, a number of their Cabinet colleagues protested the economies proposed in the name of fiscal orthodoxy. They found particularly grating the projected cuts in unemployment benefits, and it was upon this contentious point that the Labour government divided and fell. Great was the consternation of his former colleagues, and bitter their feelings, when MacDonald returned at the head of a coalition National government staffed and supported by many of Labour's political foes. Although they conspicuously failed to preserve the gold standard—the only task which united the diverse coalition—the National government nonetheless secured a landslide victory in the general election of 1931. In that election the Labour party, with three of its respected "Big Four" in the coalition camp, was unable to offer an adequate explanation of the late Labour government's actions, let alone a clear understanding of an economic alternative to the new government's policies. Possibly Oswald Mosley, a vigorous advocate of expansionist economics, would have presented a better case than Labour's remaining leaders, had Mosley not already himself left the party because of the Labour government's refusal to try out his own proposals for combating unemployment. In the event, however, Labour fared disastrously in the October election: the party constituted the smallest parliamentary opposition since 1832. Once again an allegedly radical Prime Minister governed with a parliamentary majority not of his own party.

MacDonald had no difficulty in accommodating himself to whatever policies the Tories desired, although in short order several leading Liberals retired from the coalition, unable to accept the bilateral agreements on tariffs concluded with the Commonwealth countries at Ottawa in 1932. A year later the government tacitly repudiated the war debt owed to the United States. Since Baldwin's negotiation of a debt settlement a decade earlier had been widely received as evidence of Britain's determination to restore her pre-war position, so her inability to meet its terms—whatever the justice of the American claims—symbolized economic decline. But few, of course, were troubled by symbolism, especially at a time when the reality of unemployment affected between three and four million people. Despite the initial advances of the New Deal in America, the National government continued to rely on the operation of "market forces" to ease unemployment; Britain's recovery, not surprisingly, was slow and grudging.

In the second Labour government, MacDonald had yielded the Foreign Office but continued to play a role in the formulation of a conciliatory policy. The depression undercut the era of international amity; Britain's turn to Protection was typical. Yet as

Europe grew more competitive and nationalistic, MacDonald continued to voice platitudes of peace. Despite Japanese aggression in the Far East, he refused to invest the League of Nations with anything more than moral force—one of his few remaining points of agreement with the Labour party in the early 1930's. Aversion to the bloody carnage of 1914–1918 still ran high: though the degree of pacifism (which was in all but a few cases of a conditional rather than absolute variety) can easily be exaggerated, there was no desire to return to the trenches of France and Flanders, nor, for that matter, to embark for the desolate wastes of Abyssinia. Thus the National government, with Baldwin assuming the premiership in 1935, opted for a negotiated settlement of the dispute between Abyssinia and Mussolini's Italy—at the decided expense of the former. The British government was shocked—and, briefly, even shaken—by the public outcry which greeted the Hoare-Laval pact. The public had taken all too seriously Baldwin's electoral pledge to support the cause of the League of Nations, which had condemned Italian aggression. In undertaking what was viewed as a commitment, Baldwin had won from Labour at least a portion of the pro-League vote in the general election of 1935. Though Labour's fortunes recovered significantly from the rout of 1931, Baldwin won a majority of the votes cast—the last such case in modern British history. Hoare had to be sacrificed to the public clamor, and Baldwin thereafter was all the more resolved to a policy of noninvolvement in Europe, which he would gladly have seen join Atlantis under the waves of the sea. Mussolini's victory in Africa, Hitler's reoccupation of the Rhineland, the Spanish Civil War—none of these portentous events could shake Baldwin's belief that England had to go her own way. The League of Nations faded from the scene, its possibilities going unrecognized save in Labour's ranks. Where Labour would now support rearmament on behalf of a League policy, the party resisted the National government's rearming on behalf of national ends. For such a purpose Baldwin's government in fact rearmed—slowly—after 1935, with the driving force supplied by Neville Chamberlain.

When Chamberlain succeeded Baldwin as Prime Minister in 1937, the menace of Nazi Germany could no longer be ignored.

The new Prime Minister believed in the efficacy of European conciliation, which involved the redress of genuine grievances. Moreover, he recognized that expensive measures of rearmament diverted national resources from domestic reform. He undertook a policy of appeasement which aimed at the inclusion of Germany and Italy in a settled, and just, European order. With the faith of a missionary, Chamberlain followed that design to what he considered its logical end—the cession of the Sudetenland to Germany as forced upon Czechoslovakia at Munich in 1938. His quest soured only in March 1939, when Hitler for the first time incorporated into the Reich lands which were not historically German. Ultimately Chamberlain succeeded only in altering the meaning of appeasement—from the redress of grievances to capitulation, at the expense of others, in the face of force. Confronted again with such force, this time directed against Poland, whose territorial integrity Britain had guaranteed in the hope of warning off Hitler, the House of Commons scorned capitulation. Spurred by Opposition and back-bench Tories alike, Britain went to war. The years of decline, with mass unemployment and a debased appeasement both sapping national strength, could well have culminated in defeat followed by a crashing fall.

Yet it would be a mistake to say that Winston Churchill single-handedly reversed the tides of history. Chamberlain's government, from which the outspoken Churchill had been excluded until the outbreak of war, had increased the pace of rearmament significantly, and planned and executed domestic defense measures in wartime. Whether the Chamberlain government could have ever seized the military initiative will never be known (though the ill-fated Norwegian expedition argues the contrary), for Hitler ended the "phoney war" by taking the offensive in the West in the spring of 1940. In the midst of that attack, Chamberlain could no longer sustain his hold in the Commons. He had signally failed to alert the British people to what they were fighting for. Whatever his faults, Churchill could not be accused of lack of leadership: "You ask, What is our policy? I will say: It is to wage war, by sea, land, and air, with all our might and with all the strength that God can give us. . . . You ask, What is our aim? I can answer in one word: Victory, victory at all costs, victory in spite of all terror; victory, however long and hard the road may be." Inspiring words, though it is likely that the Prime Minister had little idea of the costs that would be involved. And yet, even if Churchill had known those costs, can anyone believe that he would have shied from mortal combat with "Corporal Hitler"?

In addition to the direct costs of the war, Britain mortgaged her economic future to the war effort. In accepting the provisions of the Lend-Lease Act, Britain was practically excluded from the export trade: the efforts of inter-war governments to rebuild this vital sector of the economy were all but scrapped. Following upon the destruction of her physical assets, and the wartime practice of disinvestment abroad, postwar Britain would be ill equipped to pay her own way. Better a mortgaged future, though, than no future at all. At the same time the leveling features of a war-geared economy were much in evidence: labor was centrally controlled, and women were conscripted for war industries. Such Labour leaders as Clement Attlee, Ernest Bevin, and Herbert Morrison played a dominant role on the home front. Unlike their Liberal counterparts in the First World War, these men had no difficulty in accepting conditions for employment that restricted individual freedoms; but they did insist that wages be exempt from such control, and as a result the laboring classes significantly improved their economic lot during the war years. Moreover, there was general agreement that the workers could never again be treated as they had been during the worst years of the depression. They deserved basic standards of welfare guaranteed by the state. In such a spirit the Beveridge Report of 1942 aimed at the correction of poverty and unemployment, the historic ills of industrial society. A compromise document, the report assumed the continuance of a capitalist system, denying the socialist contention that the Treasury should finance a program of comprehensive social security. Thus it fell short of Labour's hopes. On the other hand, the Tories—particularly Churchill, who wanted to concentrate national efforts on the war—appeared ambivalent toward Beveridge's proposals. A back-bench MP, the writer Harold Nicolson, recorded: "The Tory line seems to be to welcome the Report in principle, and then to whittle it away by detailed criticism. . . . They also suggest that in many ways it is an incentive to idleness. . . ." The divergent views on postwar reconstruction began to emerge even before final victory was certain.

In the actual waging of the war, Winston Churchill ensured that his views would carry direct weight with the planners—as Lloyd George had failed to do in 1917–1918—by serving as his own Minister of Defense. Through the simple expedient of assuming major responsibility for British strategy in the Second World War, Churchill provided against the emergence of a latter-day Haig. Conflicts between the professional practitioners of war and the gifted amateur were far from few, but they were resolved privately —and successfully. Slow in answering the Russian demands for a second front, Churchill did not have to worry about conducting operations on a third front—against his own generals. When victory came in 1945, Churchill could rightly regard the outcome as a personal triumph.

He could lay claim as well to an electoral tragedy, which was in part of his own making. For all his greatness, Churchill rarely exhibited any grasp of the "political moment": in attacking his former Socialist colleagues in the electoral campaign, he showed no sense that they shared with him the nation's esteem. In failing to perceive the urgent need for far-reaching measures of reconstruction, Churchill appeared out of touch with domestic priorities. In permitting the Conservative party apparatus to crumble on the local level, while Labour had played a highly visible role in the constituencies, he mistook his personal popularity for support of his party. In this last regard, at least, Churchill was not alone; the Labour leaders wanted no part of a general election in July 1945 and, when it was called, felt little assurance of winning. Some observers anticipated a swing to the left, which was anyway in order after Labour's reverses in 1931 and 1935. No one, however, foresaw the dimensions of Labour's actual victory—an outright majority of 146 over all other parties. The path to socialism in England was clear. Hugh Dalton, exulting in the first division of the new House of Commons, ignored for the moment the pressing problems which confronted him at the Treasury: "After the long storm of war, after the short storm of election, we saw the sunrise. As we had sung in the shadows, so now in the light, 'England is risen and the day is here.'"

On the very next day, August 17, 1945, American lend-lease aid was abruptly terminated. Since no less a personage than John Maynard Keynes had warned that without continued American aid Britain would face "a financial Dunkirk," the nation's financial position was, in a word, grim. Even if the export level of 1938 could quickly be regained, Britain's overseas expenditures, vastly increased since that time, required heavy reduction; otherwise, adverse balances of payments would in time lead to national bankruptcy. Thus fiscal orthodoxy demanded the rebuilding of Britain's industrial plant, but the Labour party had not won the general election of 1945 on such a program. Instead, the Socialists were committed to immediate improvements in living conditions: the Labour government, in fact, were pledged to build the Welfare State. Whatever dim hopes Labour entertained of reconciling these conflicting claims upon limited resources lay in the socialist clause of the party's 1918 constitution, which pledged Labour "to secure for the producers by hand or by brain the full fruits of their industry . . . upon the basis of the common ownership of the means of production. . . ." Such nationalization of industry, it was believed, would secure higher levels of efficiency, while the "waste" inherent in capitalistic enterprise, including private profits, would be reduced. Following parliamentary approval of specific measures of nationalization, private shareholders were compensated, and control of the nationalized industry was vested in a public corporation answerable to the government only in matters of broad policy. Management remained largely in the hands of those who had performed the same role under private auspices; nor did the role of labor change—a matter much regretted by Labour's left wing. Thus did the Bank of England, the coal industry, civil aviation, gas and electricity, iron and steel, and public transport—including the railways, the waterways, road haulage, and passenger service—pass into public ownership, although the Conservatives subsequently legislated the return of several of these industries to private ownership.

Nationalization proved no cure-all for the nation's financial woes: increasingly, Labour's program was justified in terms of providing social services to the populace. Even before nationalization, the rails and the mines, in particular, had ceased to be profitable enterprises in Britain; curiously, if socialist ideology had not happened along, something akin to nationalization would have had to be invented by the capitalists themselves.

Clement Attlee's government was more successful in creating, and funding, the Welfare State. Because of widespread public acceptance of the Beveridge Report, Labour encountered only moderate opposition in legislating protection against the uncertainties of life in an industrial society. Benefits providing against unemployment, sickness, or industrial injury; old-age pensions; free medical care for all; supplementary benefits easing the financial strains of pregnancy and burial, stretching as it were "from womb to tomb"—not only did these various provisions exceed the *desiderata* of the Beveridge Report, but they were also to be funded by the Treasury, and not through private insurance societies. The strongest opposition came from the medical profession, which had every chance to influence the long-overdue reform of the medical system. At the eleventh hour the medical fraternity dug in its heels and voiced bitter criticism of the proposals brought in by Aneurin Bevan, the radical and combative Minister of Health. Sensing the strength of popular support, Bevan, the most formidable Labour spokesman of the time, had little difficulty in meeting the medical profession's arguments head-on and winning the day. What was too often obscured in the rhetorical flourishes of parliamentary debate was the general measure of agreement that, in Britain, the time for a planned society had come. No one knew better than Churchill that the war had been won by planning; he and his coalition colleagues had no reason to doubt that reconstruction would require any less active a role on the part of government. Viewed in perspective, Labour's approach—featuring a detailed planning of reforms in social security, health, education, and housing—represented no break in continuity but rather a dramatic extension of the pattern of recent British history.

None of this, of course, eased the burden upon the Treasury. Though planning and controls were well known from the war, rationing was much more disagreeable in time of peace. Yet the government, deferring to the need to rebuild the country's export industries, sharply restricted domestic consumption both by rationing and tax controls. Thus wartime deprivation was followed by planned austerity in peacetime: though the psychic imperative of war was lacking, rationing was extended to such basic foodstuffs as bread and potatoes. Since planning now incorporated the Keynesian concept of full employment, unemployment was no longer a problem. Yet the anomaly of good wages and full employment being unable to restore the physical fabric of English life proved both daunting and discouraging. As the recognition of Britain's economic plight deepened in the United States, the worst mistakes of the inter-war years were avoided this time around. Lend-lease goods actually consumed in the war years were written off; the Anglo-American loan agreement of 1946 stipulated a 2 per cent interest charge upon a principal of $3.75 billion, terms considered generous by the American negotiators. Nonetheless the British were grieved that their disproportionate economic sacrifices to the common good were not rewarded by an interest-free loan; the patron-client relationship between America and Britain, apparent since General Eisenhower had assumed command of the combined military forces, annoyed many Englishmen. But Britain simply had to bear such patronage, as the disastrous economic setback of early 1947 made clear.

1946–1947, Britain's worst winter since that of 1880–1881, placed unparalleled strains upon an economy which, despite the infusion of American and Canadian loans, was not self-sustaining. Confidence in the pound declined when, in July 1947, it again became convertible to dollars. The American Secretary of State, George Marshall, recognizing that war-ravaged Europe was in mortal peril of economic and political collapse, had already, in June, proposed unprecedented American economic aid. Because Ernest Bevin, Labour's Foreign Secretary, immediately recognized the import of Marshall's remarks, Britain took the lead in organizing the European Recovery Program, or the Marshall Plan, as it came to be called. Since Bevin and his colleagues were anxious to secure American involvement in Europe, they consciously accepted a role of dependency in the Anglo-American alliance. Faced with a variety of problems in the tottering British Empire, Britain's leaders reasoned that the counterweight of American presence in Europe was needed to prevent Western Europe from sliding behind the Iron Curtain. American economic aid eased Britain's immediate crisis, though in 1949 the pound was nevertheless devalued from a par value of $4.03 to $2.80. Whatever the advantages of devaluation, particularly in stimulating exports, such an action was in part a confession that Great Britain was unable to regain her pre-war financial position. Against the success of the Labour government in bringing about the Welfare State must be placed the rather dismal scene of an economy sadly faltering. Success and failure, security and austerity, marked the conclusion of Britain's heroic years.

The millennium had not come with Labour's accession to power. Disillusionment with the rigors of austerity undercut the party's appeal to those middle-class voters who had opted for Labour in 1945. In addition, the Conservatives had spent their unaccustomed years in opposition to good advantage. Party organization was strengthened; at the local level Tories deployed full-time party agents in twice as many constituencies as did Labour. Under R. A. Butler's guidance, the Conservatives not only accepted the broad lines of the Welfare State but transformed their acceptance into a party program. In the general election of 1950, Labour's majority in the Commons was reduced to six MP's; about the only thing then settled was the need for another election in the near future. Although in 1950 Attlee's government had sufficient confidence in economic recovery to terminate Marshall Plan aid ahead of schedule, the political momentum had passed to the Conservatives. Fissures in the Labour movement widened: the Socialist left, never enamoured of Ernest Bevin's foreign policy, reacted against defense expenditures inflated by the Korean War. When the new Chancellor of the Exchequer, Hugh Gaitskell, proposed charges for spectacles and dentures under the hitherto-free National Health Service, the issue of rearmament versus social services divided the Cabinet. In April 1951 Aneurin Bevan angrily left the government, along with several less well-known ministers, including one of the youngest and most promising, Harold Wilson.

All signs thus pointed to Conservative electoral success in 1951. Yet the swing was not great. After the election the Tories held an overall majority of seventeen seats in the Commons, though Labour had actually polled some 200,000 more votes than the Conservatives, which reflected Labour's strong support in heavily working-class constituencies. In the campaign, Winston Churchill distinguished the two parties in a manner since fashionable with Tory speakers: the choice between Conservative and Labour was that between a ladder, on which everyone could rise, and a queue, in which everyone was obliged to take his turn. At the age of seventy-seven, Churchill still sought recognition of his ability to lead Britain in peace as in war: "It is the last prize I seek to win," he confessed with a candor that would have pleased Disraeli. Whether Churchill's heroic virtues were required in a time of continued reconstruction is doubtful, but in fact much of the Tories' domestic program was placed in Butler's able hands. The Prime Minister's own preoccupation was foreign policy, as it was to be with his long-time heir apparent, Anthony Eden, who succeeded Churchill in 1955. Continuing Conservative rule was assured by the gradual easing of austerity—in 1954 a decade and a half of food rationing finally ended—and the internal divisions of the Labour party, although "Bevanism," as the more militantly Socialist position was called, did not make serious parliamentary inroads.

Though Churchill did not further the orderly retreat from Empire undertaken during Attlee's administration—begun with India's independence in 1947—in no sense did he attempt to reverse that process. Nonetheless Britain was determined to remain in the Middle East because of the area's strategic importance and, even more significant, the oil without which a modern industrial state cannot function. To preserve her position Britain had only to work with the Arabs, but historically she was committed to the creation of a Jewish national home in Palestine. As a result, since 1917 Britain had pursued contradictory policies in the area, which made her the target both of Zionist zealots and Arab nationalists. Conspicuously, the least successful aspect of Bevin's foreign policy had been the Middle East; far from solving the problem, Labour's years in office had served only to reveal the basic lack of military force which Britain could muster in support of whatever policy (or policies) her government might adopt. Military weakness did not deter Eden, however, when Egypt began to make a bid for leadership of the Arab world. Following Santayana's dictum that those who cannot learn from history are condemned to relive it, Eden proceeded to learn—precisely the wrong lessons—from the years of appeasement nearly twenty years in the past. Seeing in the figure of Nasser a close parallel to Hitler, he concluded: "It is important to reduce the stature of the megalomaniacal dictator at an early stage." When Nasser nationalized the Suez Canal Company, with compensation for the shareholders, Eden set into motion the course of events which led to Britain's invasion of Suez. In what Anthony Nutting, an informed Foreign Office minister, has since characterized as a "sordid conspiracy," Britain used the Israeli military attack on Egypt, which in fact had been planned by Britain and France in collusion with the Israelis, as an excuse for intervention. When this hypocritical design was disowned by Britain's major ally, the United States, Britain's military force once again proved insufficient to implement the ill-chosen policy. The shame of military withdrawal was followed early in 1957 by Eden's own departure from government; his long years of promise were thus tarnished by the Suez debacle. Eden's resignation may well have eased the shock of defeat in Britain, as public opinion had in the main resented withdrawal rather than the invasion. Yet in the Middle East the last gasp of imperialism discredited the Western powers generally and opened the way to a new pattern of power in the then undeveloped world. Nutting's words are apt: "We had sown the wind of bitterness and were to reap the whirlwind of revenge and rebellion."

Despite international decline, the fifties proved an increasingly prosperous decade domestically for Britain. Though the long-range problem of the balance of payments went unsolved, real wages rose significantly. No British government would give absolute, unquestioned priority to economic growth, as had happened in West Germany in the postwar years of the German "economic miracle." In fact there was nothing miraculous about the German economic recovery, but the British populace evinced no interest in sacrificing real wages or full employment to economists' concerns for the future. Eden's successor, Harold Macmillan, proved himself a consummate politician in recognizing and responding to the dominant mood of the nation. In 1957, while warning against the perils of inflation obscured by prosperity, he had pointed out that the people "have never had it so good." In 1959 the Tories entered the general election on precisely that note: "You're Having it Good—Have it Better—Vote Conservative." Increasing numbers of voters accepted the materialistic logic and rewarded the Conservatives with a third consecutive electoral victory, unknown since the halcyon Liberal days before the First World War. Labour's dejected analysis of the returns centered upon the loss of professional and white-collar support, which in 1945 had looked to Labour as the party of the future; then, too, there had been considerable working-class defections. Such was the skepticism about the party's future that Penguin Books published in 1960 a paperback asking the stark question, *Must Labour Lose?*

Confronted with Labour's declining fortunes, left-wing Socialists began to agitate outside the bounds of parliamentary democracy, which they considered unresponsive to both domestic and international problems. As recently as 1956 the young playwright John Osborne had attacked the enervating complacency of the Welfare State: "I suppose people of our generation aren't able to die for good causes any longer. We had all that done for us, in the thirties and forties, when we were still kids. There aren't any good, brave causes left." That generation soon discovered a cause, however, and mobilized to achieve it in the ranks of the Campaign for Nuclear Disarmament. To their contempt for the "independent deterrent," as the British nuclear arsenal was euphemistically described, the forces of the New Left added scorn for the materialism and politics of their elders. Though they scored no clear political breakthrough, the questioning attitude behind their actions gave birth to a wave of satire; together, the probing forces of satire and dissent provided a useful corrective to the complacency which goes hand-in-hand with affluence.

Ironically, the left's quest for unilateral disarmament served to revive the standing of Labour's leader, Hugh Gaitskell, who showed both political courage and skill in resisting the rising tide of unilateralism within the party. Vowing to the 1960 party conference, which had overridden his objections, to "fight and fight and fight again," Gaitskell within a year had brought Labour around to his point of view. In the process he had begun to take on the look of a national leader. Meanwhile, Harold Macmillan had staked his political fortunes upon British entry into the Common Market. Despite attempts to rebuild the Anglo-American relationship, which had been badly compromised in 1956, Macmillan concluded in 1961 that Britain's future lay in Europe, rather than as an Atlantic power. Yet the nation remained dependent upon the U.S. to maintain her role as a nuclear power. After tortuous negotiations with the "Six," which served to enhance the political standing of the Conservative's Edward Heath, General de Gaulle denied Macmillan's vision, and France vetoed Britain's application for membership in the Common Market. Thus the road to economic recovery, passing through Europe, was blocked off to the country which had, in the forties, defended above all others European independence.

If international gratitude is short-lived, so too was the degree of political omniscience ascribed to "Supermac" in the early sixties. Compounding the Common Market rebuff to Macmillan was the domestic scandal centering around the Secretary of State for War, John Profumo, who added to an indiscreet private life public lies to the Prime Minister, the Cabinet, and the House of Commons. *The Times* of London chose to view Profumo's behavior as an indication of a general moral crisis, rooted in the Tory quest for material affluence, which had brought the nation "spiritually and psychologically to a low ebb." The political damage was real, though the inherent importance of Profumo's sexual adventures can easily be exaggerated. One need only recall Macaulay's century-old comment: "We know no spectacle so ridiculous as the British public in one of its periodic fits of morality." Nonetheless Macmillan's control of the government's security services had been unsteady, and his hold on power weakened as a result.

Despite these reverses, the Conservatives did remarkably well in the 1964 election. Led uncertainly by the aristocrat turned commoner, Sir Alec Douglas-Home, the party yielded power only grudgingly to Labour. Gaitskell, however, had not lived to see the triumph for which he had paved the way. In his place stood the former Labour dissident, Harold Wilson, with a minuscule majority of four but quite undaunted by the constraints upon his power. In conscious imitation of the Kennedy style, Wilson embarked upon a vigorous program of legislation within the first hundred days of his regime. A man for the moment (how else reconcile his statement while in opposition, "I myself have always deprecated appeals to the Dunkirk spirit as an answer to our problems . . ." with his credo as Prime Minister, "I believe that the spirit of Dunkirk will carry us through . . . to success"?), Harold Wilson rose splendidly to the challenge of government. So successful was he in dishing the Tories, particularly Douglas-Home, in the House of Commons, that the Conservatives were quickly forced to look about for a more formidable leader. In 1965 Edward Heath was elected—the first Conservative leader chosen in a democratic fashion by the entire parliamentary party. If their hope was to secure a Tory copy of Harold Wilson—fierce in the cut and thrust of debate, maddeningly optimistic whatever the setback, cocky, charismatic—the Conservative MP's chose poorly. But just possibly the Tories did well, consciously or not, in selecting a leader whose style has since proved closer to Gaitskell's than to Wilson's.

Wilson's artful politicking produced a harvest of Labour votes in 1966: he increased the party's majority to ninety-eight and even generated speculation about Labour's "natural majority." Once again, however, the success story of a government was sapped by economic deterioration: Wilson, his attention fixed upon the political symbolism of a stable currency, rejected fiscal advice to devalue the pound and insisted instead upon a policy of deflation. The result was that economic growth was restricted, not spurred; pockets of unemployment developed; and trade union leaders grew uneasy about government proposals to relate wage increases to increased productivity. Nonetheless, Wilson's measures did not sustain international confidence in the stability of sterling as a world currency, and the Labour government were constrained to devalue the pound, to $2.40, in November 1967. Thereafter the Treasury passed into the charge of Roy Jenkins, the most successful of the Labour ministers, who followed a financially orthodox course. Addressing himself to the perennial problem of Britain's unfavorable balance of payments, Jenkins brought the nation's accounts into solid surplus for the year 1969.

For his part, Wilson had not done so well with the trade unions, which successfully resisted the government's attempts to legislate an incomes policy. Moreover, union leaders demanded inflationary wage settlements, quite in excess of advances in productivity. In a time in which every man seemed to look to his own interests, Wilson turned his eye from inflation and instead fixed upon public opinion polls which indicated an astonishing recovery in Labour's fortunes. Calling the election for June 1970, the Prime Minister hoped that a low-key campaign would see him through to an unprecedented third consecutive personal victory. Most observers expected it would, for his opponent, Heath, had failed to generate much excitement; only at the last moment did one of the five political polls indicate the possibility of a Tory triumph. Though disenchantment with Wilson's government had long since set in, and spiraling prices threatened family incomes, Wilson expected re-election on the novel political theory that he represented "the lesser of two evils."

Evidently the electorate did not agree, for it returned a Conservative majority of thirty-seven MP's, which by past standards appeared sufficient to see Heath through five years in office. In the Tory election manifesto, reappraisal and reform figured prominently. Thus Heath will once again press the British application for Common Market membership; perhaps, at least in Europe, Great Britain will invalidate the judgment of Dean Acheson that she ". . . has lost an Empire and not yet found a role." Certainly, should Britain enter the Common Market, her links to the Commonwealth will be weakened, and relations with America altered as well. Reappraisal likely will extend all the way to Keynesian economics: Heath's government must confront the question whether sustained economic growth, full employment, and unhampered collective bargaining are fully compatible in the Britain of the 1970's. With the emergence of such a question, it may well be that an era—perhaps the Age of Keynes itself— will have ended in the humdrum but surprising election of 1970.

Part 1

YEARS OF DECLINE, 1919–1939

TOWERING IN stature above his colleagues, Lloyd George was widely—and properly—credited with the revival of Britain's flagging war effort and the strengthening of her resolve to defeat the Central Powers. Yet his accession to the premiership in December 1916 provided much more than a morale boost for Britons. An innovator, Lloyd George had reorganized the governmental structure, elevating his own office above the historic notion of the Prime Minister as the "first among equals." In the process he exposed his regime to two quite different dangers: criticism of a vaguely constitutional sort from those who feared the imposition of a "presidential" system in England, and opposition of a decidedly political nature from those Liberals who felt that he had treated his predecessor, H. H. Asquith, badly. Whether or not the primary responsibility for this is correctly traced to Lloyd George, its effect upon the Liberal party was shattering.

In addressing himself to the pressing postwar problems that W. P. Crozier outlines in his article in this section, the Prime

Minister had to gain the approbation of a coalition government and of a Tory-dominated House of Commons. From the first, his options were reduced, for the national leader in wartime found himself dependent upon the votes of his historic enemies. Whatever Lloyd George's hopes for the future, the present had to be taken on a day-to-day basis. Opportunism became the necessary style of government. Yet a number of his colleagues were deeply disturbed by the Prime Minister's apparent cynicism as well as by his policies. Looking upon Lloyd George rather as Gladstone had viewed Disraeli—that is, as a corrupting force in public life—Stanley Baldwin, uncharacteristically, played a leading role in the 1922 Conservative withdrawal from the coalition. As is evident in P. W. Wilson's article, Baldwin was the product of an entirely different milieu from the Celtic radicalism of Lloyd George. Even as Chancellor of the Exchequer in Bonar Law's government, Baldwin likely did not foresee further advancement, but, more important, even if he did, his vision was shared by few. Winston Churchill, disillusioned with the Liberal party but not yet again a Conservative, contemptuously referred to the new ministry as "a government of the second eleven." Yet Churchill's judgment of political rivals, then as later, was poor, and he failed to perceive that Baldwin embodied Britain's turning away from heroism. The nation's quest for "normalcy" found a parallel in the America of Warren Harding. The political "magic" of the Welsh wizard was as out-of-date as the idealism of Woodrow Wilson.

Succeeding Bonar Law in 1923, Baldwin's own fallible political judgment was never more evident than in his decision to go to the polls in December on the issue of Protection. Lacking a parliamentary majority, Baldwin deferred to J. Ramsay MacDonald, less than a decade earlier a pacifist and the most hated man in England. As Labour leader MacDonald did not bring bolshevism to Downing Street: he headed, after all, a minority government, dependent for parliamentary survival upon Liberal support. Even more important, the new Prime Minister lacked a revolutionary temper, as his own words indicate: "Continuity and the evolutionary method are normally the appropriate ways for applying conflicting party principles to the imperfections of the world." Concerned in the main with foreign policy, Mac-Donald's views, expressed in this collection, point the way to the era of Locarno—essentially an extension of the concept of "normalcy" to the sphere of European relations. Of greater consequence, MacDonald invested the League of Nations with little more than moral suasion, lest it become another alliance bloc. Though he was to leave the Labour party broken in 1931, when "normalcy" had already had its day, MacDonald's aversion to the use of force bedeviled Labour and the nation when the fascist challenge had to be faced.

The inter-war years in Britain have been characterized as a period of decline. Yet for contemporaries the decade of the twenties had been a time of prosperity at home and conciliation abroad. To be sure, the problem of structural unemployment, evident to such an expert contemporary as Sir Philip Gibbs, scarred the domestic scene; what Gibbs did not know was that unemployment had in 1928 reached a low point for the inter-war years, nor could he foresee that the situation would soon deteriorate rapidly. While Gibbs's palliative of emigration for the problem of unemployment may sound strange to our ears, the idea was a current one: viewers of "The Forsyte Saga" will recall that Michael Mont's maiden speech in the House of Commons paid tribute to "Foggartism," the systematic emigration of the young to the Dominions.

Whatever the limited possibilities for emigration, the onset of the depression outpaced them: the long lines of the unemployed, shuffling in their queues but going nowhere, demanded a more radical remedy. Though Labour assumed office again in 1929, that government was conspicuously unsuccessful in dealing with the problem, despite urgent pleas for dramatic corrective measures from within the Labour movement. When a financial crisis broke in England in August 1931, the Labour government disintegrated; its successor, the coalition National government, proved to have no better solutions to the problem of unemployment, and "life on the dole" persisted well into the decade for millions of working-class Britons. Radical critiques of governmental inaction were voiced in several quarters. From the left came the cockily phrased but measured arguments of John Maynard Keynes, who maintained that state planning, on a massive scale, could control the economic situation. Since the publication of his *General Theory of Employment, Interest and Money* in 1936, Keynes's views have remained influential.

Fortunately of short-lived significance was the rightist critique of Oswald Mosley, who had resigned in disgust from the Labour government in 1930 and then moved across the political spectrum to lead the British Union of Fascists. Mosley argued that English fascism, though modeled on continental versions, would go its own way; nonetheless, Harold Callender's carefully questioning interview indicates that traditional English liberties would not long have survived the establishment of the corporate state. Discredited both by domestic violence and events abroad—Hitler's Blood Purge followed by a few days the publication of Callender's interview—Mosley's movement lost strength. Still, the fears of 1934 that the country might lapse into what Stafford Cripps called "country gentlemen's fascism" were real enough; they were rooted in the malaise of that troubled decade.

The lack of success in dealing with continental fascism on the part of MacDonald, Baldwin, and Neville Chamberlain is well known; what is often ignored is the fact that these men were representative of the national mood of their time. Churchill's masterly philippics have obscured the deep conviction shared by most of his contemporaries that war was to be avoided, in Anthony Eden's words, "at almost any price." D. W. Brogan, subsequently a distinguished historian, conveys in his article the all-important sense of what the English people thought they were doing, and why, in the 1930's. Though in 1937 Britain's "boundaries of endurance" were both elastic and remote, the shame of Munich and the continual aggressiveness of Hitler led, two years later, to a geographic definition of these limits. When Poland was attacked in September 1939, Britain went to war. Brogan correctly anticipated that Britain would not conduct "a dignified policy," but he foresaw as well that national unity would be forged. Possibly the shared sense of national disgrace accounted for the grim mood with which Great Britain went to war, described by Sir Philip Gibbs in terms of its vivid contrast to the national euphoria of 1914. Whatever the source of the grimness, whatever the reasons for the national unity—both were to be called upon in full measure during the long course of the Second World War.

The Future of Lloyd George

by W. P. Crozier

WHAT IS Lloyd George's future? It is the absorbing question of
politics in England. He has achieved an unparalleled position.
He has climbed, or rather leaped with agile bounds, to the top
of the ladder, displacing brusquely some of those who stood in
his way. He has fought Mr. Asquith in his single-seater and Mr.
Asquith has indubitably "crashed." He gave the vote to women
and the women voted for him, not because of what he gave
them, but, as an Asquithian Liberal said with bitterness, because
he is the only politician of whom they had heard.

The "little Welshman," in fact, has grown to a political
colossus. It has become almost a joke that no great issue, no
crucial difficulty, can be settled without him. It is said that in
one great newspaper office a standing headline in the largest type
is kept—"The Premier Intervenes"—for use in the latest stage
of the very latest crisis; and cynics declare that the parties to
every great dispute insist that it shall go through its ceremonial
and appointed stages until at last "the Premier intervenes" and
hey, presto! the rabbit emerges from the pocket handkerchief.
Whether Lloyd George is magician or charlatan, a brutal dictator

From the *New York Times Magazine,* February 23, 1919, copyright ©
1919, 1947 by The New York Times Company.

or a benevolent autocrat, a camouflaged Tory or an unrepentant Radical, at all events for the moment he is the "top dog." And probably that satisfies his deepest instincts, for he is, above all, ambitious, competitive, pugnacious.

In foreign politics we see his way fairly clear before him. We have our British Junkers, who are content that the world after its bath of blood should relapse again into its state before the war, but outside their stiff-necked ranks the wish is almost universal that Mr. George should "stick to Wilson." There is good reason to believe that that is what he means to do. It is not, of course, that he will whittle down any British interest that is intrusted to him. It is not that he will fail to give due support to the just claims of our European allies. We believe that President Wilson, like ourselves, appreciates the national timidities of European States—of England about her security on the sea, of France about her eastern frontier, of Italy about her unprotected Adriatic coast.

But England, all the best that is in it, believes that only in Mr. Wilson's principles can be laid the foundations of a just and permanent peace (however difficult it may be to settle each particular case by an application of them) and that her own best contribution and safeguard lies in the sincere co-operation of the English-speaking peoples.

There are many "official" Liberals who dislike and mistrust Mr. George, but every time that he shows himself in sincere alliance with Mr. Wilson he wins them back toward his side. For to many Liberals, be it remembered, Mr. Wilson has long been more of a leader than any one of their own chiefs.

Domestic politics are threatening and men wonder whether Mr. George is strong enough to ride the storm. Since the armistice of Nov. 11 a large part of English industry has been almost paralyzed. Great firms and combines which would normally have given orders in that time to the tune of half a million sterling have ventured only a few thousand pounds. They fear that when they have bought at the present high rates there will be a sudden break in prices, and for such loss there will be no compensation recoverable from the Government; they are skeptical enough of securing any compensation even on stocks which they held at the time of the armistice and may now sell at a loss. They dread also the complete uncertainty which at present surrounds the "on-cost" of goods in respect of labor charges.

The labor world does not know its own mind. It demands a reduction in the number of working hours (at the old wages) and, having obtained it, straightway demands another. How is it possible to quote prices or make contracts if one does not know from one week to another what the wages cost will be? So industry stops, and, with an eye on Mr. George, the commercial world inquires what the Government proposes to do to restart the machine. And, though industry is stagnant, the workers ask and obtain more wages, so that prices rise, the reluctance to place orders grows, and stagnation is increased. Meanwhile, demobilization quickens, the workers are flocking back to industry, and unemployment grows. Soon we shall all be looking anxiously for the old formula "the Premier intervenes."

Mr. George's political position is difficult. The fact is that he did far too well at the election. The Unionist wing of the coalition has a clear majority in the House of Commons, and the Labor Party, the largest single party outside the coalition, is in formal opposition to him. Where will Mr. George stand on the delicate and critical questions affecting labor that will come before his Government? Or, take one single point of the greatest political importance—the reform of the House of Lords. Almost everyone believes that if Mr. George does not succeed in carrying through Parliament a radical program of social reconstruction, the popular current will set very strongly toward the Labor Party. Good judges predict a Labor Ministry at the next election.

But a Labor Ministry will have ideas about land and capital and all economic questions which will be very unpalatable to the Tory Party. What more natural, then, than that the Tory Party, which now controls both houses of Parliament, should desire so to reform the House of Lords (which is at present hamstrung by the Parliament act) that it will present a bulwark against the coming Labor Government? But Mr. George is a democrat, a son of the people, a House of Commons man. Where will he stand in any attempt to recast the Lords and strengthen it against the House of Commons? That is a snag, and a big one.

There are others. There is Ireland, where no one knows from one day to another what will happen, especially when the Sinn Feiners have failed, as they will fail, to get their cause a hearing at the Paris conference. It is perhaps a pity that they should fail, since the application of "self-determination" would certainly result in the temporary partition of Ireland, and without some such temporary expedient there is little prospect of Nationalist Ireland ever obtaining the home rule which is her right (since it is on the statute book for Ireland undivided). Mr. George and his Government are believers in "self-determination," but Nationalist Ireland will not have a solution that savors of partition; they are Home Rulers by their own admission, yet the state of Ireland, which is never without its paradox, prevents them from applying the only home rule which is practical politics.

The bill for the war is coming in. In his election campaign Mr. George fell in with the popular demand that Germany should be made to pay the whole cost of the war. But most thinking persons believe that it will not be practicable to exact £24,000,-000,000 from Germany, and that when the bills for simple "reparation" have been paid, there will be little more that can be drawn from Germany. That is certainly the view held by high quarters in France, where the suggestion that every power was to make an equal claim to war costs was followed by intimations, unofficial, but firm, that "reparation" to France and Belgium must come first and not be prejudiced by the more general war costs of the other Allies.

But if Germany is not going to pay the British war bill, who is? Clearly the British taxpayers. But which taxpayers? Those that have more or those that have less? Increasing numbers of people, reflecting on the enormous burden of debt and its danger as a cause of popular discontent, have come to advocate a levy on capital as a means of wiping out quickly and completely a substantial portion of the burden. Bonar Law, always honest and outspoken, was rash enough in his first utterances to express approval of the project. But his party friends looked frostily upon him and he has since been much more circumspect.

To judge from his antecedents, Mr. George would be in favor of the levy. But behind him in the Commons will sit the unbroken phalanx of Tory opinion which has already forced Mr. Law to a discreet withdrawal. Will Mr. George come out in favor of the levy, will he be able to enforce it on the Tory Party (the party which will pay) and so attenuate the general burden? It is difficult to see any alternative scheme which is half so hopeful. There is no doubt that the electorate has been led by Mr. George to expect that Germany will pay. If she does not, it will certainly expect him to find some easy method of removing at least a large part of the debt from the masses of the people.

Finally, though Mr. George is "top dog," his position has its difficulties. He is not yet leader of the Liberal Party. It is reported among both coalition and noncoalition Liberals that he has definitely decided to summon a meeting of Liberal M.P.'s and be elected leader. He can do it, and if he does he will succeed. But it will be at the cost of a formal split in the party, for the Asquithian organization, embittered by its crushing defeat at the polls, will take up arms against him. Nevertheless, he may emerge triumphant. If he can impose a progressive program on the Tory Party or if he breaks with them because they will not have it, in either event he will have a strong claim to the leadership of the whole Liberal Party. He has not at present got either the House of Commons or the Ministry that he desires. If he could lead a party composed of the great mass of the Liberals, moderate Labor men and democratic Tories like Lord Milner and Lord Richard Cavendish-Bentinck, it would suit him well. As for the rank and file of the Asquithian Liberals, they desire to see the schism in the party healed. Mr. Asquith is discredited. Mr. George has his chance. He needs all the support that he can get, for labors of Hercules await him.

A Typical British Chancellor

by P. W. Wilson

WHAT INTERESTS ONE about Stanley Baldwin, Britain's Chancellor of the Exchequer, who has been talking things over at Washington, but has not lent himself to anecdote, is not so much the man nor yet his high office, but rather the type—the very influential type—to which he belongs. Drop into the parlor of any British bank, run your eye over the directorate of any railway or shipping concern in that land of shopkeepers, and you are sure to be greeted, politely, even pleasantly, by some gentleman, suave, smiling, yet seriously sympathetic, whose name, had Providence so cast the lot, might have been Stanley Baldwin.

Of such a stock was Peel the severe, was Gladstone the thunderous, both of them bred in business, without being of it. Of such a stock was Ruskin the seer, and Robert Browning the poet, men of inherited means, accustomed to every comfort, and thus born the masters of their own circumstances. Baldwin might have been a poet, a bishop, or, like William Wilberforce, an artist in philanthropy, but politics seemed more obvious, and as his father before him sat in Parliament, there was no obvious excuse for changing the custom of the family.

From the *New York Times Magazine,* January 28, 1923, copyright © 1923, 1951 by The New York Times Company.

True, there were now no pocket boroughs, but what—considering babies and bazaars—might be called out-of-pocket constituencies were still to be had—safe regions like the Bewdley Division of Worcestershire, where the cabbages, the cows and the carrots are still strictly Conservative in opinion, where the Methodist chapel does not really rival the Established Church, where the radicalism of the village pump is corrected by the toryism of the village pub, and squirearchy with hierarchy, as fixed for all time by that matrimonial theologian, King Henry VIII, survives —world without end—so be it. To somebody or other one must touch one's cap, and to touch it to Stanley Baldwin was as simple and as inexpensive as to pull a forelock to anybody else.

Worcestershire, therefore, not being Wales and predatory, but only near Wales and tory, Stanley, in 1908, triumphantly floated into Parliament, which became the station that, according to the Prayer Book, God had called him into. Since that proud day there has been in Europe the trifling rumpus which some hysterical historians call a war, but in the Bewdley Division of Worcestershire the trees still grow, the hats are still touched, the pub still fights the pump, and "Stanley's seat in the House" is still safe. His private address, moreover, is still Eaton Square, while even sterling, in which are reckoned his investments, almost stands at par.

About such Englishmen there is a serious reserve. They don't want to be clever. They make no pretense to be brilliant. Often they lack or conceal imagination. But it takes much to get them excited. With an ease which is apparently effortless, they preside over some commercial undertaking, nonchalantly accepting their profits and their losses, neither boasting of the one nor bewailing the other, but taking each day as it comes and muddling through it—never dreaming that in their existence there could be such a thing as failure. They do not announce success; why should they? Success is what invariably they assume. One does not announce a normal temperature.

It is the public schools of England that produce this type. Baldwin went to Harrow, answered the roll call and wore the required straw hat that is held by elastic, not under the chin like a girl's, but a. the back of the skull, where nature provides

Harrovians with a mental groove not vouchsafed to the rest of us, which phenomenon Sir Auckland Geddes, being an anatomical Ambassador, might investigate. From Harrow, Baldwin passed on to Trinity College, Cambridge, so completing what in England corresponds to the grand tour.

Harrow and Cambridge taught him that, while business is business, business is not the whole of life. Outside of business are the home, the wife, the two sons and the four daughters, and sundry grandchildren. There are books; there are sports; there are public duties. The ease of these men in business is due to the fact that they master business instead of business mastering them. If they lift the burden, it is only to throw it off. They have hobbies. They take exercise. They worry more over a dog than over a dividend. Of an evening at the fireside they can forget. At the week-end they can enjoy a novel. And when old age draws on they can retire from the firm altogether without the feeling that the time has come to die. In themselves are resources which outlast the fascinations of finance.

Against the English public school—what Americans would call a very private school indeed—much may be urged. Endowments intended to give the poor boy a chance have been, in too many cases, shamefully appropriated by the exclusive and the rich. But having said all this, the fact remains that these schools have made to citizenship an enduring contribution. Within itself, such a school is a pure republic. At Eton neither wealth nor birth counts for anything, but only what a boy is, what he does, what he is ready to suffer. Individuality has full play, but at every point it is overshadowed by the loyalty demanded for the institution. The advantage to one's self is steadily held subordinate to the common good. The deepest instincts of right and wrong are expressed in the decisive phrases—"good form," "bad form," "really" and "not quite the thing."

The code may not be and, indeed, is not altruism. But it embodies certain fundamental virtues, a sense of fair play, of personal honor, of rectitude, on which, save for inevitable and tragic exceptions, one may absolutely rely. There are countries where no oath is more binding than the formula "on the word of an Englishman." On the other hand, this very prestige has its occasional perils. There have been cases—few and far between—where it seemed outrageous to question the honor of a man, who, though a rogue, was so sure of himself, so indifferent to the sordid haggling of the market, so remote from greed and want that suspicion was kept at arm's length. The guineapig director who sold an honored name to allure the simple investor has been, therefore, at times a great abuse. And only this year a financier of the highest standing, with clients at Court, fled in an airplane from his liabilities, was brought home to face his trial, and after a wretched disclosure of extravagance over wine, women and song was sentenced to seven years' penal servitude. About the severity of the law in such a case—despite social influences—there was permitted to be not one moment's question. Public school judges could not have been more severe on this public school delinquent.

At the public school the rich man's son meets boys of whom nine out of ten will have to earn their own living. Here are the civil servants of the future, the doctors, the lawyers, the clergy, the teachers, the soldiers and sailors, the actors and artists. The leisured class thus hears and shares the call to service. To be a prefect, to sing in the choir, to play on the team, is an honor. The question today is thus not whether the public school man is available, but whether he is any longer wanted. Despite the impoverishment of the aristocracy and of the middle class, despite the increase of school fees, the public schools and universities are crowded as never before.

But what is to happen to their pupils? Few of them are now going to India. With the broader franchise and the rise of labor, there is not the chance that there used to be in Parliament. The Church is underpaid. The inflation of the Civil Service has been much abated. What shall we do with our sons?

Why is it that Eton and Harrow and Winchester have lost, in a measure, their old supreme influence? It was inevitable. The great schools started things. But any school could be inspired by the example. The qualities which were revealed at Harrow permeated the Boy Scouts, the Girl Guides, the football leagues, the regiments, the battleships. England could not be so governed without learning to govern herself. And about Baldwin and his set, there was this to be remembered: Between man and man they are honorable. Their word is their bond. But between class and class their sense of equity is sometimes challengeable. The agricultural laborer, for instance, has often had to complain of treatment that no stretch of language could call a fair deal. And in the test case of Ireland the ethics of the public school entirely broke down. At Uppingham, reckoned to be one of the most enlightened of these institutions, there was in the old days a debate, led by Lord Crewe, as the distinguished visitor. The subject was home rule, and the only boy who took the side of Lord Crewe was his seconder; which boy was told that, as an act of hospitality, he had to. It was the illiberalism of such a herd-mind that drove a public school man like Erskine Childers into a revolt more Sinn Fein than Sinn Fein itself.

Apart from the war and the disruption of parties, there was no reason why Stanley Baldwin in particular should have been selected as Financial Secretary to the Treasury and then promoted to be Chancellor of the Exchequer. For a time he had been Bonar Law's unpaid private secretary. Moved by sentiments also voiced on behalf of "the City" by Reginald McKenna, he threw in his lot with the Die-Hards and against Lloyd George. But there were others as capable, as well informed, as excellent in speech as he who might have gained the limelight.

At the Carlton Club, at the United Universities, even at the Athenaeum, you may find at any time statesmen of this calibre. But in dealing with the debt owed by Great Britain to the United States, Stanley Baldwin has this supreme advantage: He is not simply himself—he is also England. His country is the only axe that he has to grind. He has no reason now to think of votes or ambitions. His ambitions must be more than fulfilled, and he has had the votes. In him Secretary Mellon is thus addressing not a politician but a nation. What Baldwin says is what the House of Commons and the country will be sure to echo. His point of view is the point of view which the country insists on having presented. He is a plenipotentiary. He is the unanimous and comprehensive spokesman.

And one is glad of it. For this is not a situation that requires genius. No legerdemain will pay a debt of four and a half billion dollars. Over such a liability as that you cannot split hairs or bargain. The eternal equities are called into play, and will not be denied. Here is music that must be faced, every note of it, banknotes included. Is it to be 4½ per cent interest, or what interest is it to be? Is payment to be rendered in twenty-five years, or what term of years should be fixed? These are questions which the man in the street, all over the world, can understand and answer for himself.

Finance—even high finance—is not and should not be turned into magic. A statement on finance that fails to be simple cannot be wholly sincere. No honest mind ever elaborated into an abracadabra the theorem that twice two is four. The budget speeches of Gladstone, which glowed with eloquence, were never other than lucid, and the bigger the figures with which a Finance Minister has to deal, the fewer should be his embellishments of them.

The speeches made today in the House of Commons by a Chancellor of the Exchequer when he presents his budget are in the main typed statements, prepared by the Treasury and delivered by the Minister as the mouthpiece of unalterable arithmetic. Whichever party were in power, the substance of such a speech would be the same. The only Chancellor who dared to humanize the statistics was David Lloyd George, and he at the moment happens to be avoiding bullfights in Spain. Stanley Baldwin will thus handle his budgets as calmly and as coolly as he handles any other piece of business. For several years he will repeat a loudly applauded performance, after which encores he will begin to wonder whether, after all and despite all they say, it is not rather nice to be a Viscount. With a magnifying glass the atlas will be studied in order to discover some village the name of which has not been hitherto employed to ornament a peerage, and when the remote hamlet has been found it will become the living mausoleum of a charming but disappearing personality. Viscount This-or-That will appear unrecognized in Who's Who, but what in Heaven's name will have happened to that fellow Baldwin.

His rebellious heir will desperately promote a bill to enable him, as a commoner, to follow in the footsteps of his father, escape the gilded chamber, continue in the House of Commons, and remain, as Sir William Harcourt used to put it, "an English gentleman." But the only evil that Stanley Baldwin ever did will then live after him and from the father to the son, into the third and fourth generation, that Viscountcy, when it comes, will inevitably descend. It will last for centuries after the United States has been paid by Great Britain every cent that she owes.

MacDonald Points the Way to Peace

by J. Ramsay MacDonald

IT WOULD BE interesting to study the metal that goes into the coinage of phrases that have become popular currency and are passed around as accepted wisdom. A certain proportion of truth there must always be in it, but a vitiating amount of error is generally found in the alloy. This is the case with the subject upon which I have been asked to write.

The nature of the work of the British Foreign Office is special. The nation in its world relations is weak or strong, insignificant or influential, by reason of its standards of honor, the spirit of its policy, its consistency and reliability. Whatever presents its will as wavering and uncertain destroys its influence and lowers its prestige. In domestic administration we have to deal with the traditions, the habits and the opinions of our own people; in our foreign relations we have to deal with those of others. In domestic affairs we and our wills alone are concerned; in foreign affairs, the convenience and policy, the opinions and will of foreign Governments have to be taken into account.

Hence it is that the Foreign Office has stood all by itself

From the *New York Times Magazine,* January 4, 1925, copyright © 1925, 1953 by The New York Times Company.

among the departments of State and has called for the exercise
of more personal discretion than they. Hence, also, it is that
the public instinctively expect that its work should be immune
from the partisan conflicts in which they are apparently willing
that the work of other departments should be mauled. And so,
when some one gave expression to the doctrine of continuity of
foreign policy, the phrase became enshrined among the common-
places of political wisdom.

The truth in it was both obvious and salutary. A country that
changes its foreign policy with the winds of popular feeling
must be a weak country and will soon have no friends and no
allies. A country whose foreign policy depends upon the turns
in party fortunes will be nothing better than a person of whim-
sical affections. A country whose political parties consider that
as a matter of party rectitude they must undo or alter the transactions which their opponents have had with foreign powers will
be the cause of world unsettlement and can neither work out a
destiny for itself nor lead in world causes. These facts are plain
unto commonplace, but in view of the voracity of partisanship in
these days it is not waste of time to remind it that foreign policy
should be guarded against its appetite.

I take it for granted that every Government and every Opposition, in the interests of the nation, should ever set before themselves the duty of keeping foreign affairs out of the ordinary partisan arena and should strive to give foreign policy the impress
of national concern. But, in practice, serious limits are found to
the doctrine. If followed absolutely it must mean in the end
that the Foreign Office would be controlled by a permanent
bureaucracy, whose personnel would change in the course of
nature, but whose personality could never change. It also would
mean a constitutional alteration in the position of the Foreign
Secretary, who should then become a quasi civil servant and
ought not of necessity to resign with a change of Government.
The old Russian Foreign Office was a model of such an organization, and that could only fit into a system of government which
was personal and despotic throughout and made revolution inevitable. We need not dream of such madness here.

Another set of facts must also be taken into account. Britain is governed by representative public opinion, and that necessitates the existence of party. In every democratic State there must be groups of men—in normal times, not more than two—who, holding different conceptions on some great body of political or social opinion, regard national well-being from different angles. The difference must have some effect on foreign policy, and, even when aims and purposes are the same, it will point to different roads and different methods of approach. Sometimes it will amount to more than that, and the holders of two opposing conceptions, both honestly pursuing what they consider to be national interests, will follow irreconcilable policies, absolute alternatives.

The late Labor Government, for instance, were as much concerned as their predecessors regarding imperial defense and national security, but they rejected the proposal to build a naval base at Singapore, being convinced that it was a menace to the peace and safety of the empire. It also happens now and again that the country rejects policies that have been pursued, and newly chosen majorities are compelled by a democratic verdict to make a sharp break with the past.

This means that whatever wisdom is in the doctrine of continuity, it must not run counter to the essential conditions of public opinion ruling through representative government, and to that extent the country must take the risk of an occasional break in continuity, because that is the alternative to the much graver risk of pursuing fatuously a policy which it condemns.

In spite of these limitations, however, the general policy of continuity has a broad scope of usefulness. The vast bulk of Foreign Office work involves no question of principle. Here continuity ought to rule, the touch being all that is altered. Moreover, even in making the changes which difference in party outlook implies, it is well that statesmen should have some rules to remind them that he who can transform things without violence and sharp breaks is possessed of a higher degree of greatness, and is more likely to do good that will last, than he who demands for his work a clean slate, and can write nothing in history except what begins a new volume, or at least a new chapter.

The crudest form of diplomacy is that of revolutionary forcefulness, scrapped treaties, the clean slate. Small States can indulge in it, and second-rate States play with it, but first-class powers cannot risk it, and cannot afford it. Such a power must win confidence for steadiness and consistency, and any political party which damages that confidence may tickle and please its followers for a time and during the hot days of a crisis, but the reputation of the country will have to pay heavily for demonstration of party probity.

How happy would a British Foreign Minister be, for instance, who could tear up much of what has been agreed about reparations: and yet, though he may be worried by the watchfulness required if reparations are to be prevented from seriously damaging our trade, how foolish would he be if, of his own will and without the consent of allies with whom we had signed the bargains, he were to end them all by a stroke of his pen and bring chaos, ill-will and suspicion to help him out of his difficulties.

Rather, he must impose upon himself the duty of persuading his allies to come to new and better agreements, and of meeting the evils which he inherited by new expedients which he devises. Continuity and the evolutionary method are normally the appropriate ways for applying conflicting party principles to the imperfections of the world. The characteristics of the revolutionary mind are to be studied in their evil effects in far more subtle manifestations than riots and civil war.

A Tory Government with a ponderous majority may, in the exercise of an absolute will, do more to strengthen the spirit and the mood of Bolshevism in the country than ten years of ranting and frothy communist propaganda.

If, however, we think of continuity as a virtue and a wisdom in itself, we lose grip on reality and wander into the confused and misty realm of words. What is to be continued? Plainly not a policy by reason of its having been begun, but a policy only in so far as it promotes national well-being. Our demand for continuity in foreign policy has, therefore, to depend on two things: the wisdom of the evolutionary, as opposed to the revolutionary method, and the amount of common agreement that exists in what should be the general objective of our foreign policy. Are the conditions under which the country is to retain its place in the world, and maintain its safety and honor, so plain that we may reasonably expect that the several political parties will stand upon much common ground regarding them?

It is difficult to say, but I know that many adherents of all parties hold similar views on propositions like the following, and were general agreement come to regarding them no change of Government need either encourage our enemies to bluff and squeeze or make our friends doubtful as to whether or not they could continue to rely upon us.

We should undertake no further commitments, especially in territorial administration. Our resources of power and capacity for this work of unknown responsibility are already heavily drawn upon, and ought to be relieved as much as possible. No cooperation with foreign States should involve us in military alliances, and we should, with absolute rigidity, refuse to be parties to an apparent solution of the problem of national, or, indeed, international, security by the formation of such alliances. What happens in this respect within the next twelve months is almost certain to settle not whether there may be another war, but whether that war is inevitable.

But a negative position on this is not enough. We must without reserve champion the League of Nations, not as an alliance which, should a war break out, would secure victory to one side, but as a combination of nations to create the machinery and the obligations necessary to maintain peace.

These two views are contending for mastery at the present moment, and it depends almost solely upon us which is to prevail and whether security is to be built upon the sands or upon a rock. In working this out there may be moments when the risks we have to run will be disquieting, but we have subscribed to the obligations contained in the League of Nations Covenant, and without delay we shall have to make up our minds whether when we signed that Covenant our tongues were in our cheeks, or whether we knew what we were doing and committed our honor to do it should need arise.

In the whole of our policy we should aim at bringing all the nations of Europe into the companionship upon which we are to depend for the fullness of our international life—including trade and commerce—and peace. Nor can we leave the American Continent out of account. Here again there is a growing agreement among those who know the American mind. America can render invaluable service (and has done so) in pacifying Europe, but we must pursue our policy with America or without it, leaving the initiative to America itself and trying to influence it neither by European smiles nor frowns. American cooperation will be measured by the character of our European policy, and if we are wise we shall leave it at that.

Such an outlook upon the world and such a conception of the part that this country has to play among the nations allow full scope for party differences and yet permit all parties to present statements of national policy which, in spite of variations in light and shade, emphasis and relative importance, modes of action and programs of action, will convey the sense of a common purpose rather than of an aimless wandering and a wind-tossed destiny depending upon newspaper stunts or party fortunes. If, however, the conditions of continuity, as I have indicated them, are but party views, and other groups of men and women will pursue different ways to different ends, there is one last consolation that we all can share. The resistance of circumstance will prevent, except upon the rarest occasions, those violent breaks and those exercises of the absolute will which damage national reputation. In reality, we need not perturb ourselves unduly about the practicability or impracticability of these phrases. Their value lies in the reminders they give us not of what wisdom is but of some of the elements of which wisdom is composed.

When the conflicting considerations of statecraft and national well-being, which an examination of this phrase summons for view, have been fully weighed, perhaps the best and the fullest verdict we can give is that in the determination of international policy two classes of people are nearly always wrong and mischievous (though even these have their uses): he who so soon as he sees something untoward in the foreign intelligence columns of his morning's paper becomes righteously indignant and wants to know what drastic action the Government has taken to show that it and himself exist: and he who never considers the consequences of what he takes to be some act of elemental justice, but believes that the injunction to do right and face the possibilities of the heavens falling means that he has no responsibility for anything that is likely to happen to himself or to others by reason of his selfish indulgence in his own sentimentality.

From either or both of these sections come the evils to the State which the demand for a continuity of foreign policy seeks imperfectly to avoid. And because I must write "imperfectly," I add another conclusion to the verdict; and that is that there is no vade mecum for Foreign Ministers, no general rules of safety or success which they should pursue devotedly and with strong nerve whether they seem on the moment to be making a mess or a success of things, but that those filling this office have only one loyalty to observe, loyalty to their country and their country's fame, and only one steady counselor upon which to lean in selecting their methods and in fulfilling their allegiance —their own good sense.

The Paradox of Britain's Unemployed

by Sir Philip Gibbs

IT IS DISTRESSING to all English folk and friends that ten years
after the war the figures of unemployment in England stand at
the tragic total of 1,250,000. For a time, last year and this, they
were reduced to something below a million—bad enough but
showing a decline. Now they have jumped again, chiefly in the
mining districts where many men have been discharged from
unprofitable pits.

What is the cause of this paralysis of manpower which
amounts to a national danger? Is there something wrong with
the spirit of England—some weakening of will power and loss
of grit, or is it the fault of the Government, or of old-fashioned
systems of industry which have not kept pace with a hurrying
time? Or worse still, perhaps, is it some inevitable law of economic facts against which there is no remedy by any kind of
wisdom or readjustment to new conditions?

One curious thing about this industrial condition in England
is that, apart from the black belt of unemployment, the state
of the working classes has never been so good. Wages are higher
in many trades and businesses throughout the country. Since

From the *New York Times Magazine,* September 16, 1928, copyright ©
1928, 1956 by The New York Times Company.

the war whole classes which were on the poverty line or below it have been lifted up to a fair level of comfort and prosperity. Even in the slum areas, where there is still a lot of over-crowding, the foulness of life, such as Charles Dickens described and as I knew it before the war, has practically disappeared.

Go down to the East End of London now, into streets where it was unsafe to walk when I was a boy, and you will see decent and respectable people, crowds of neatly dressed girls with shingled hair and stockings that look like silk, and none of the old hideous squalor. It is a real transformation of life. So, too, with the "lower middle classes" as we used to call them—small shopkeepers, clerks, mechanics, printers, and factory workers.

During the last ten years their way of life has been enlarged and made more agreeable. They have moved up in the social sphere. Many of them own their little houses—which are spoiling the beauty of the old estates now broken up for building plots. They drive small cars. They have a "wireless" over the chimney pots and a gramophone in the parlor. They approximate to the American standard of living among their own class and are not far behind. Outside the unemployment areas—mostly in the North —there is every sign of prosperity in England and it is a real prosperity based on industrial activity, the position of London as the exchange center of the world, and a healthy distribution of money.

How is it then that 1,250,000 people are out of work and that according to the report of a recent commission, which makes gloomy reading, many hundreds of thousands of men in England have no prospect of ever finding work again in their old employment?

One cause is to be found in the condition of the coal-mining industry upon which the economic prosperity of England was largely based in the Victorian era. At one time English coal was bought in all the ports of Europe at a high price, and this created a heavy carrying trade for the mercantile marine, stimulated shipbuilding, and gave advantage to many other industries, including steel and iron. But now there is an overproduction of coal. Germany is competing with English prices. France, whose mines were destroyed in the war, has reorganized them and is increasing her output for export purposes. Other countries have developed water power and electricity. The navy is using oil. Motor lorries are carrying traffic formerly taken by the railways whose coal consumption is reduced.

Meanwhile, the mining areas of England vastly increased their payrolls during the war so that afterward they found themselves employing a working population far in excess of profitable results at a time when it was necessary to close down poorly paying pits and to install labor-saving machinery. It seems certain that 200,000 miners are not wanted and never will be wanted again. That is a tragic sentence of doom for some of the finest men in the world, strong in character as in body, with nothing wrong in them.

That slump in coal has affected other industries, and especially, perhaps, shipbuilding and the mercantile marine. It checks the flow of prosperity and many activities in other trades. Steel and iron are not doing well partly because of a Franco-German combination which is formidable in competition. Europe has not yet recovered its purchasing power—the war has still to be paid for—and many old markets of England are in a poor way of business. The miracle is not that England has suffered so much but that she has suffered so little, and that in ten years since the war her industrial and financial recovery has been so rapid, so strong, and so progressive in spite of all these drawbacks.

It is not a sign of bad government or of an enfeebled people. On the contrary, looking back on the past ten years I for one must admit that our spirit has stood the test of many ordeals and that the wealthy classes especially—the old landowners and the people with inherited possessions—have stood the racket with considerable self-sacrifice. Income tax, super tax, and death duties have broken up their estates, and their fortunes have been reduced at least by half, which after all is rather a whack even for a rich man. There are less than 100,000 people who pay super tax and it is they who have borne the biggest burden of prodigious expenses following the war. It is partly their money that has been redistributed into the pockets of the poorer classes, with good results. But still there remains that frightful disease in the industrial life of England—those 1,250,000 unemployed.

One possible cause of the evil has been pointed out by Professor Keynes, who wrote "Economic Consequences of the Peace" and is nearly, if not always, right in his prophecies of woe, though he irritates many people by being so cocksure. In order that the pound "might look the dollar in the face"—an admirable ambition, no doubt—the British Government, and especially the Bank of England, which tells the Government what to do, as an oracle delivers judgment, adopted a rigorous policy of "deflation." That is to say, they restricted credit, covered their paper money by a gold reserve, tightened up their loans, economized in public works and frowned on the rival policy of stimulating trade by "cheap money."

This drastic deflation was, perhaps, too rapid and too rigorous. Mr. Keynes says so and he seems to know. Certainly it was the cause of the miners' lockout which led to the general strike two years ago. It just made the difference to the selling price of coal for export purposes, annihilating the British chance of competition with foreign rivals in world ports. It has also checked industrial activity, as the restriction of credit always does.

Well, that is an argument which I am not qualified to enlarge upon in a dogmatic way, but there seems something it it. Anyhow it seems stupid that with strong men waiting to work and with the material of their work at hand—steel and iron and cement—and with people wanting houses and bridges and roads and machines, there should be a slowing down of national activity for lack of credit from the banks. For labor and material are the securities of wealth. They are wealth itself, surely. In addition to this restriction of credit, industry in England is severely handicapped by excessively heavy rates on land and property, from which the Government offers relief next year, and unemployment is increased by what is called the "rationalization" of business, which means more efficiency in methods by amalgamation and the scrapping of poorly paying concerns.

There is one vital weakness in the social structure of English life which, in my opinion, is the chief cause of this inability to find work for healthy men. The land has largely gone out of cultivation. The old English peasantry has passed away, owing to free trade and the industrialization of the nation, which depends upon the export of manufactured goods in return for food supplies which come pouring in from Canada, Australia, the Argentine and other agricultural countries. Small farms in England can hardly be worked at a profit. Ex-service men who went on to the land after the war were speedily ruined. It does not pay to grow wheat.

The arable land of England is fast being turned to grass. This means that there is no sound basis upon which men can plant their feet and upon which the superstructure of civilization should be built. France, with her protective tariffs, maintains an agricultural population and her peasant farmers are the most solid foundation of her well-being. There is no unemployment in France because there is always work on the land for sturdy young men, and foreigners have to be engaged as factory hands, builders and craftsmen. Unfortunately England decided half a century ago to live by merchandise and manufacture, and agriculture languished while her cities grew big.

In present conditions it seems certain that England cannot absorb at least 1,000,000 of her working population into industrial life. They must either go on being supported by the State, living miserably on the "dole"—which should be called unemployment insurance and is their legal due—getting more and more demoralized, losing heart and spirit, and becoming embittered, or they must get out of England and find work elsewhere. That verdict must also be given in the case of the younger generation now approaching working age with not enough work to go around—unless there is some radical alteration of industrial conditions. That is an even greater calamity.

In the sister nations of the British Empire—the great Dominions of Canada and Australia, especially—there is room for 10,000,000 workingmen, and then another 10,000,000. Why, then, for goodness sake, is there all this difficulty in transplanting that surplus 1,000,000 in England? The question must be answered squarely. In the first place, many of the young men now unemployed do not want to leave England. They like England. Some of them fought for it. They do not see why they should be put out. And they have grown up in English civilization, with its city life and its cinemas and its lighted streets, and its little comforts and amusements. They do not see the fun of going out to lonely spaces, cut off from all their friends and exiled from all that seems to make life pleasant. They are not used to the land. They have no love for it. They are the children of an industrial nation. That is one aspect of the problem.

The other aspect is equally difficult. The Dominions of Canada and Australia are not playing the game, in my frank opinion. They are not making things easy for English settlers. So far they have done very little to cooperate with the British Government in any big plan. In Australia many of the trade unions are definitely hostile to English immigrants because they believe that they tend to reduce wages and spoil the labor market. Their Government sets up hard-and-fast rules insisting upon agricultural experience and rejecting willing men of good character and strong physique who are eager to come out and do any kind of work.

I can give one case which came within my own experience and is typical, I am told, of the general attitude. Last year I had a letter from a young miner who had been out of work for two years. It was a very striking letter showing great intelligence and force of character. Instead of wasting his time during this period of unemployment he had gone every day to a public library and had followed a definite line of reading—history, the great masterpieces of fiction and elementary science. That was to keep his mind from rusting and to prevent himself from being demoralized. But he was desperate to get out to Australia and do a man's work on the land. He was physically fit—as strong as a horse—and not afraid of rough labor. Could any man be more suitable as a pioneer? But Australia House [the headquarters of the Australian Commonwealth in London] had turned him down because he had had no agricultural experience. They turned him down again when I took up his case and put in a plea for him. Australia, which depends for its future greatness on getting a large population of good stock, turns down the finest quality of English manhood on a red tape rule. That is not playing the game.

It is short-sighted and stupid and disloyal to the mother country.

In Canada it is not much better. The Canadian Government looks askance at English immigration and is not cooperating with any great enthusiasm in any big policy of settlement. Certainly there have been disappointments and failures. Men who have gone out to Canadian farms from England after the war have not stayed on the land, finding the Canadian winter intolerable and the hardships too great, and have drifted down to the cities and the lure of the lighted streets. The disease of civilization is hard to cure.

But there is a way to avoid the terrors of loneliness which seems to be the chief handicap of the city-bred man. That is to devise a big scheme of community settlement. Why not take 200,000 miners with their families and establish them in groups and small townships in touch with shops and cinemas and reading rooms and the amenities of modern life? These men of the mining population in England are as good human stuff as one could find in the whole world—good natured, hardy, self-respecting, full of generous qualities and humor, and hard workers if they get the chance. They are of the same stuff as their forefathers who built up a great empire.

It is disastrous and damnable that for lack of leadership and some big plan administered by a big mind their lives and spirit should be wasted on the "dole." Is there no big mind in Canada or Australia, but only little pettifogging men swathed in red tape and putting up niggling objections to a vision of the future? England can do nothing in that way without a call from the Dominions and a leadership from their side. One cannot send out men to other peoples' lands where they are not likely to be welcomed.

Failing some big imperial scheme there are methods of readjustment in England which may do something to relieve the unemployment situation in some degree. These populations of out-of-works are too stationary. The mining crowd especially seems to be tied to their own geographical areas. As the Industrial Commission points out, groups of them ought to be drafted into districts where there is need of labor, by railways facilities and arrangements made by the Board of Trade and Government grants. Then again there ought to be training centers for the teaching of agriculture and technical trades in order to provide the families of miners and other industrialists with a chance of escape from employment which has become hereditary, so that the son of a miner must be a miner or is lost in the scheme of life.

The English trade union system with its forms of apprenticeship and its jealousy of the open door has created a kind of cell-like structure of industrial life which prevents access from one trade to another. A builder cannot be an engineer. A house painter if he loses his job cannot switch over to bricklaying. Once a carpenter always a carpenter, because one cannot get a trade union ticket in another branch of work. This prevents a free flow of labor and stabilizes unemployment in distressed industries. The remedy for that is not the smashing of the trade unions, which are essential for the protection of labor and wages, but Government training centers with free apprenticeship—though in making that suggestion I am probably going beyond my range of knowledge.

At least I am sure of this—there is no immediate hope of eliminating unemployment in England except by a big movement of emigration, reducing the population by something like 1,000,-000. On the other hand, this surplus population of unemployed people is not a proof that England is going downhill or is generally in a desperate way—although for a time I thought so. There are more people in active employment than before the war, and the general prosperity of the working classes—if they are working—is on a higher level.

In all the business of exchange, banking and general finance London has regained her position as a world center. Many industries are doing well. New trades have been established. Fortunes are being made. There is still a lot of wealth in the country and the immense burdens of the war are at least being faced and borne by those who have to pay. Money on the whole is better distributed among the various classes in spite of inequality and injustice which are inescapable, perhaps, in modern life and human nature.

That dark blot of unemployment spoils the picture, and is beyond doubt a national danger of sinister importance, but it looks to me as though it were due to an increase in population which cannot be absorbed into an industrial system, which has reached its limit of expansion, until new markets are opened in other countries of the world.

Critic of Britain's Muddling Through

by Harold Callender

AS THE economic depression has dragged on, the British public, as distinct from the scholars and specialists, has become increasingly aware of that remarkable person, J. M. Keynes. He is to be heard occasionally in lecture halls or over the wireless. His comments on events may take the form of letters or articles in The Times, of economic-philosophical essays in The New Statesman, of contributions to those illuminating reviews issued by the great British banks, of elaborate theoretical treatises, of short and incisive pamphlets, or of brief articles in the popular newspapers whose readers are numbered in millions and in whose somewhat lurid columns the academic Mr. Keynes seems strangely out of place.

But Mr. Keynes is quite at home in all these media. He has written a treatise on money which few but specialists can read; he has also written biographical studies which are literary achievements and interpretations of economic happenings which are so lucid and untechnical that—as he himself might put it—even statesmen can understand them.

He is at once an outstanding economist and an uncommonly

From the *New York Times Magazine,* September 17, 1933, copyright © 1933, 1961 by The New York Times Company.

gifted writer. Were he not renowned for his monetary studies he would still be distinguished as an essayist and a dissector of historical personalities. His political writings have the same grace of style, the same provocative sharpness, the same caustic wit as his elucidations of economic topics; and he can discuss the balance of trade or the principles of central banking in such a way as to make these somewhat forbidding subjects positively entertaining. This combination of learning with a certain lightness and vivacity—and also a kind of intellectual aggressiveness— lends to Mr. Keynes a distinctly Gallic quality.

It may be this temperamental trait, quite as much as his academic training and his official experience, that accounts for the fact that Mr. Keynes has been one of the most persistent and devastating critics of the British habit of "muddling through." In this familiar phrase is expressed the British distrust of theories and theorists, the ingrained British empiricism which prefers to rely upon instinct and tradition rather than upon logic, the British disposition to look only as far as the immediate future and to be guided from day to day by events. Priding themselves—not without reason—upon the comparative success of this method in the past, the British have been wont to elevate it into a principle and to regard the habit of "muddling through" as almost a national virtue.

Mr. Keynes, to whom theories are neither so alien nor traditions so venerable as to most of his fellow-countrymen, would prefer intelligent planning to muddling. He would prefer to control events rather than to follow them, and he is convinced this could be done if the lessons of economics were applied in the sphere of practical politics.

He offers the interesting spectacle of the academic mind challenging the so-called practical mind—that of the bankers, the Treasury and the Bank of England—on the ground that it is not really practical at all but is so immersed in details and so fettered by precedent and tradition that it does its job in a very bungling manner—that it merely "muddles through." "The abstract thinking of the world is never to be expected from persons in high places," wrote Bagehot. "The administration of current transactions is a most engrossing business, and those charged with them are but little inclined to think on points of theory, even when such thinking most nearly concerns those transactions."

This is much the way Mr. Keynes feels. Economics, he has said, "is a true science, capable perhaps of benefiting the human lot as much as all the other sciences put together." But the "practical" men, suspicious of theories and somewhat dazzled by the scintillations of the academic mind at its best, cling to the familiar routine and the traditional ways of thinking.

Thus Mr. Keynes personifies the radicalism of the scientist in contrast to the conservatism of the man of affairs; the experimental spirit of the laboratory as opposed to the cautious precepts of the counting room; the venturesomeness of the scholar, sure of his thesis and longing to prove it, as against the unyielding skepticism of the conservative banker and politician.

The antithesis is striking, especially in England, where banking and business are conspicuous for their conservatism and government for its unimaginativeness. If Mr. Keynes is impatient, caustic and at times a bit dogmatic, this is due no doubt to the strength of the forces opposing him—to the power of British tradition and to the British distrust of intellectual brilliance.

Mr. Keynes's case is weakened by the very cleverness with which he advances his arguments and by the ridicule he lavishes upon those whom he attacks; for the British like neither cleverness nor vehemence and are not a little suspicious of both. If Mr. Keynes is inclined sometimes to overstate—as when he calls economics a true science—the reason may be found in the ardor of his convictions and the resistance they encounter. And if he praises the Roosevelt recovery program, it is because, in its fundamental assumptions, if not in all its methods, it represents an attempt to carry out in America the policies which Mr. Keynes has been vainly preaching in England for years.

In advocating expansionist measures and in criticizing the Treasury for practicing rigid economy when what was needed, in his view, was greater expenditure on public works, Mr. Keynes was not speaking altogether as an outsider. He passed thirteen years of his life in the civil service. At the age of 30 he was made a member of the Royal Commission on Indian Finance and Currency. During the war he drafted the agreements for the interallied loans. At the peace conference he was the principal representative of the Treasury and sat with the Supreme Economic Council. His civil service career came to an abrupt end, when, disapproving of the reparation clauses, he resigned and soon thereafter published his "Economic Consequences of the Peace," a severe indictment of the treaty of Versailles. The book, which proved prophetic, made him famous and thenceforth he remained before the public as an untiring critic of the economic arrangements of the treaty and of the monetary policies of his government.

Mr. Keynes was only 36 years old when he denounced the peace treaty and—with all the contempt of the youthful scholar for the compromises of elderly "practical" men—depicted brilliantly and mercilessly the drama of Versailles and the leading figures in it. But he was already a veteran in public affairs, having entered the civil service upon graduation from Cambridge at the age of 23. His father had been Registrar of Cambridge and Keynes had been reared in an academic atmosphere. After the peace conference he returned to Cambridge as fellow and bursar but as chairman of a life insurance company and of The Nation (later merged with The New Statesman for which he still occasionally writes) he retained his contact with London and his position as lecturer to the British public and the world at large, as well as to university students.

Now 50, he still seems young. He retains the verve and audacity, the disrespect of tradition, even something of the cocksureness, of youth. For this there is an excellent reason: His criticisms have largely been confirmed by events. It is no reflection upon his public spirit to suspect that as he makes his sharp thrusts at bankers and politicians he takes a not unnatural joy in discovering that his aim has been true. The accuracy of his forecasts is an impressive bit of evidence in support of his contention that economics is, or could be, a true science.

There is youthful animation in his movements as in his writing. He is tall and slightly stooped, but the motions of his head are quick and his eyes flash in a singular manner as he talks. He seems to like making startling remarks in an entirely matter-of-fact tone.

He writes in a terse, concentrated style which is the height of lucidity and with an easy grace which enhances the occasional touches of humor and irony. "It is the method of modern statesmen," he wrote in 1921, "to talk as much folly as the public demand and to practice no more of it than is compatible with what they have said." In the two years following the peace Mr. Lloyd George was "protecting Europe from as many of the evil consequences of his own treaty as it lay in his power to prevent, with a craft few could have bettered; preserving the peace, though not the posterity, of Europe, seldom expressing the truth, yet often acting under its influence."

Mr. Keynes describes the bankers in general as "impeccable spinsters" who "profess a conventional respectability that is more than human" and consequently are "the most romantic and the least realistic of men." Mr. McKenna favors an expansion of credit, but what can be expected of Montagu Norman, governor of the Bank of England, "moving within the limitations of his own mentality"? When the bank chairmen discussed Britain's prospective return to gold in 1925, Mr. Keynes wrote this comment:

"Once more the bank chairmen have held up for our inspection their financial fashion-plates. The captions vary, but the plates are mostly the same. The first displays marriage with the gold standard as the most desired, the most urgent, the most honorable, the most virtuous, the most prosperous and the most blessed of all possible states. The other is designed to remind the intending bridegroom that matrimony means heavy burdens from which he is now free; . . . that it will be for him to honor and obey; that the happy days when he could have the prices and the bank rate which suited the housekeeping of his bachelor establishment will be over—though, of course, he will be asked out more when he is married; that Miss G. happens to be an American, so that in future the prices of grapefruit and popcorn are likely to be more important to him than those of bacon and eggs; and, in short, that he had better not be too precipitate." This, be it remembered, from an economist discussing a monetary question and summarizing the weighty pronouncements of half a dozen bank chairmen.

To a collection of writings published two years ago Mr. Keynes gave the title "Essays in Persuasion." They embody his comments and warnings during ten bewildered years. They were, he said, "the croakings of a Cassandra who could never influence the course of events in time." Mr. Keynes is nothing if not persuasive. What he has tried to persuade his readers is, above all, that "the economic problem . . . is nothing but a frightful muddle, a transitory and an unncessary muddle. For the Western world already has the resources and the technique, if we could create the organization to use them, capable of reducing the economic problem, which now absorbs our moral and material energies, to a position of secondary importance."

Like the practitioner of preventive medicine, he strives to make his profession unnecessary, or at least of minor importance. He looks forward to a time when the economist will have no serious problems to solve and little or nothing to do; when "the economic problem will take the back seat where it belongs, and the arena of the heart and head will be occupied, or reoccupied, by our real problems—the problems of life and of human relations, of creation and behavior and religion."

"Assuming no important wars and no important increase in population, the economic problem may be solved, or be at least within sight of solution, within a hundred years." The economic problem, the struggle for subsistence, "always has been hitherto the primary, most pressing problem of the human race" and indeed of the whole biological kingdom "from the beginnings of life in its most primitive forms." But it is not necessarily the permanent problem of the human race. If he applies his intelligence so as to solve it, man will be faced "for the first time since his creation with his real, his permanent problem—how to use his freedom from pressing economic cares, how to occupy the leisure which science and compound interest will have won for him, to live wisely and agreeably and well."

Thus the economic problem should not be overestimated; nor should "other matters of greater and more permanent significance" be sacrificed to its supposed necessities. The economic problem should be "a matter for specialists—like dentistry"; and "if economists could manage to get themselves thought of as humble, competent people, on a level with dentists, that would be splendid!"

Thus the Cambridge Cassandra is not such a pessimist as he might have seemed. His dire warnings, and the impatient and almost bitter tone in which they are uttered, spring from his consciousness of the enormous contrast between what is and what might be; between the spectacle of idle men, idle capital and human want existing together, and that of a state of life—almost within our grasp—in which there would be no economic difficulties worth bothering about.

If he ridicules the bankers and politicians, it is because he feels that, in their blindness to the vision vouchsafed to the economist, they are preventing the solution of the economic problem and deferring the day of deliverance. If he condemns the traditional orthodoxy of the Bank of England and the Treasury, it is because he longs to see the economic muddle cleared up expeditiously and finally by those who know how.

Mr. Keynes has often changed his opinions. The pages of one of his recent books, he said, were littered "with skins I have sloughed." But his conviction remains that the Western world can solve its economic problems if it goes about it in the right way. "The obstacles to recovery are not material. They reside in the state of knowledge, judgment and opinion of those who sit in the seats of authority." It is a matter of human intelligence and will. In a passage reminiscent of William James's "Will to Believe," Mr. Keynes stresses the utility of faith. "If we consistently act on the optimistic hypothesis, this hypothesis will tend to be realized."

Mosley's Creed:
A Revealing Interview

by Harold Callender

FASCISM HAS LATELY become a lively issue in England—not because it is yet regarded as a serious competitor for power but because its Blackshirt guards at a recent meeting in London freely used their fists upon those who ventured to exercise the traditional British privilege of heckling a speaker. There was more violence in one hour at this meeting than during the whole general strike of 1926. [Clearly an exaggeration: about 1,000 people received prison sentences for violence or incitement to violence in connection with the general strike, and these were but a quarter of those prosecuted for such offenses.—EDITOR] This injection of strong-arm methods into political contests, which in this country are almost invariably conducted on a gentlemanly plane of sporting give-and-take, shocked and alarmed many Englishmen.

The British Fascists until recently gave the impression that they were different from the Continental species. There seemed nothing of Nazi bluster or bullying about them. They were obviously Continental in inspiration, in vocabulary and in organization; but they seemed disposed to rely upon the normal methods

From the *New York Times Magazine*, June 24, 1934, copyright © 1934, 1962 by The New York Times Company.

of persuasion to advance their cause. To one who has observed the development of fascism on the Continent, the British Black-shirts still seem comparatively mild. Their fisticuffs, which seem so scandalous in England, are trifling in comparison with the armed strife which was a commonplace in Germany. But to the British they represent something disquietingly new in politics, something foreign and disturbing—though their followers manifest a youthful gusto which the aged and fatigued Conservative party may well envy.

If to many, fascism, as expounded by Sir Oswald Mosley, its British leader, seems much too Continental for this parliamentary country, it differs in some of its professed principles from both the German and Italian varieties.

British Fascists as a rule do not so much as mention the Jews; they do not advocate any of the socialistic measures, such as nationalization of banks, which formed such a prominent part of the Nazis' program before they came into power; they have no "racial policy" and do not, like Mussolini and the Nazis, urge their country to increase its population as rapidly as possible; nor do they, like their Continental counterparts, favor the subjection of women.

Outspoken as it is, Sir Oswald Mosley's book, "The Greater Britain," is a model of restraint in comparison with the crude violence of Hitler's "Mein Kampf." On the platform Hitler shouts and rants in strangely loose and formless German; Mosley does not strain his voice, uses few gestures and utters sentences so well constructed as to suggest that they have been carefully written out and memorized.

In a recent conversation Sir Oswald was asked particularly to explain how fascism could be reconciled with the British traditions of freedom and individualism. He answered numerous questions in a straightforward manner and at some length. British fascism, he indicated, agreed with many of the basic doctrines of Continental fascism, but hoped to advance by less drastic methods.

"You have said," the interviewer began, "that the Fascist movement in this country would be peculiarly British. Do you then repudiate the whole philosophy of liberalism, as Mussolini and Hitler do?"

"The Fascist movement here certainly will be peculiarly British but not liberal," Sir Oswald replied. "It is a mistake to confuse Britain with liberalism. The liberal spirit was a very temporary phenomenon in our history and is already dead. We repudiate its philosophy."

"In that case would you advocate the retention under a Fascist régime of all the individual liberties now possessed by the British people, such as a free press, the right of free speech, the writ of habeas corpus, trial by jury, etc.—liberties which have all been suppressed by existing Fascist governments?"

"We shall ask of the press a sense of patriotism and of national responsibility," said Sir Oswald. "We hope and believe it will be unnecessary in Britain to adopt measures which have been necessary in foreign countries. The spirit and tradition of the British press are very different.

"As for freedom of speech," he continued, "there is much confusion about this expression. It now means the freedom of a few politicians to talk at will. Fascism would provide a new outlet for the expression of the views of the masses through the corporations of a technically organized State.

"As for habeas corpus, trial by jury, etc., it will be unnecessary to interfere in any way with traditional British justice, provided fascism secures power before a social collapse comes. It has often been necessary in British history to interfere with the normal operations of the law, but we trust and believe such interference will not be necessary. We shall, however, codify and simplify the laws of England, which is now a lawyers' paradise."

"You said at the Albert Hall," remarked the interviewer, "that no real freedom exists in this country. Yet in speaking in the Albert Hall you were exercising a kind of freedom which does not exist in Fascist countries—the freedom publicly to criticize the system of government. And in your book you said: 'We shall continue to exercise the right of free speech and shall do our utmost to defend it.' Does British fascism, then, espouse free speech as a principle?"

"The Fascist State would supply a more effective medium for constructive ideas. The methods of securing free speech would be different; they would be suited to a technical system. Within the corporations the individual would be able freely to express his opinions. But controversies would assume a technical form and would not follow party lines as now. Elections would be held on the basis of a technical or occupational franchise and the corporations would be the appropriate instruments of opinion. The country would be transferred from a political to a technical system. Free speech would acquire a new meaning which it is difficult for the democratic mind to comprehend."

"But what about criticism which might be called destructive; that is, the right, now freely exercised in Hyde Park and elsewhere, to oppose the system itself?"

"We don't think it possible," was the reply, "that the country would want to change the system. But the voters would be able to change the government at fixed periods by universal franchise. The government could be criticized through the corporations and the press would be free to criticize. We are against the whole atmosphere of party warfare. New men would emerge by reason of their constructive ideas, not by reason of their skill in the parliamentary game. The politicians would be eliminated and there would be greater opportunity for expression of intelligent opinion than ever before."

"You speak of freedom to criticize within the system and through the corporations; but does fascism contemplate a static society in which opinion that seemed to conflict with the system would be forbidden?"

"The Fascist State," said Sir Oswald, "would provide for evolution at any speed. The excuse for freedom of speech is that only thus can new ideas be advanced. We should provide a better medium for new ideas; but we should not allow attempts to overturn the State, and Communists would be suppressed. We should certainly not need to ask so much of the press as our government asked during the war."

"Does this mean that you would establish permanently a control over the press similar to that which existed in wartime?"

"The degree of freedom enjoyed by the press and every one else would depend upon the degree of the crisis. We believe that by taking action in time we can avoid the necessity for the rigorous measures which were necessary in other countries in conditions of chaos."

"At Karlsruhe," said the interviewer, "a man has just been sentenced to fourteen months' imprisonment for trying to persuade a woman to vote against the German Government at the last election. Would you sanction such methods under a British Fascist régime?"

"Assuming this report to be correct," answered Sir Oswald, "what about the 3,000,000 who did vote against the government? They were not imprisoned. But our elections would be free and nobody would be bulldozed."

"Would a British Fascist régime, in your opinion, conduct elections as in Italy and Germany, where non-Fascists may not run for office, or would it allow free elections in the British sense?"

"The corporations would freely choose their representatives, and the people would vote their approval or disapproval of the government every five years. If a government were defeated in an election, the King would call upon an alternative leader to form a government. Our system would be much more flexible than Italy's; we should adapt fascism to the British character."

"In Germany, as you know, several thousand persons have been confined in concentration camps without trial, on political grounds. Would you say that such methods would form part of a Fascist policy in Great Britain, or would you tolerate them?"

"We believe," replied Sir Oswald, "that Britain will adopt the creed of the modern age before a collapse and thus avoid the rigors manifested in some degree by Fascist governments in other countries, though I do not credit all the reports of their repressive activities. The rigor of fascism is in proportion to the chaos which precedes it."

"In a lecture called 'Vom Sinn und Wesen der Nationalen Revolution,' Professor Otto Koellreuter of Jena said: 'The liberal constitutional rights of the bourgeois State lose their meaning [in the Third Reich], because State and freedom are no longer separable conceptions.' Do you accept this authoritarian conception of the State in accordance with which, in Italy and Germany, the individual has no rights which the State is bound to respect?"

"We believe in the authoritarian State," said Sir Oswald. "As I said in my book, every man shall be a member of the State, giving his public life to the State, but claiming in return his private life and liberty from the State and enjoying it within the corporate purpose of the State. We claim, first, that the individual would enjoy greater private liberty than now, since he would attain economic security; second, he would be free in his private life from the numerous restrictions imposed by democratic parliaments. The average man does not care to talk but to enjoy economic prosperity."

"To what extent is the British Fascist movement anti-Semitic?" Sir Oswald was asked. "Does it purpose to discriminate against Jews in any way?"

"There will be no racial or religious persecution under fascism in Britain. The Jews will merely be required to put the interests of Britain first."

"Both Mussolini and Hitler," said the interviewer, "while protesting that their respective countries have not enough territory, actively urge their peoples to reproduce as rapidly as possible. Do you approve this method of national aggrandizement?"

"This question," replied Sir Oswald, "involves birth control and similar problems which are no business of the State."

"Is one justified in inferring from your book, in which you oppose the 'present parliamentarism,' that you do not share Mussolini's and Hitler's condemnation of parliamentary government as such?"

"We are against the political Parliament and favor a Parliament, based upon an occupational franchise, which would be a technical instrument."

"Is there any disposition on the part of your movement to repudiate 'liberal culture' in its entirety, as is done by the Italian Fascists and the Nazis, and to seek to create a new national culture, under State control and sanction, in its stead?"

"We repudiate liberal culture and aim at a new national culture, to be attained through the spiritual revival which fascism will bring about."

"You would not, then, seek to dragoon the nation into a new culture?"

"We think the spiritual appeal will be adequate. We look for a new morality and a new psychology. The revival of the spirit must precede a change in the material environment."

"What is the likelihood that British fascism would indulge in the burning and suppression of books, as in Germany, or would exercise any such political control over the stage, the films, literature and all the arts as seems necessary to the Nazis?" Sir Oswald was asked.

"We don't want to spend our time censoring literature and the arts, but we should stop the pornographic and decadent tendencies of certain elements of modern literature. Aside from that, we should encourage the maximum of freedom of art and thought."

"The question," said the interviewer, "referred particularly to political censorship."

"No more in literature than in politics," replied Sir Oswald, "should we permit efforts to overthrow the system."

"Mussolini, in the Encyclopaedia Italiana, writes: 'Fascism does not believe in either the possibility or the utility of perpetual peace. . . . Only war raises all human energies to the maximum and sets a seal of nobility upon the peoples who have the virtues to undertake it.' Do you agree, and does British fascism agree, with this statement?"

"I understood Mussolini to mean that a flabby people might sink into decadence. He said in a later speech that the combative instinct might be sublimated in a struggle against nature. There is room enough for our energies in this struggle against nature. War is obsolete as a test of manhood; the modern test is the conflict with nature."

"Do you believe that fascism has given Italy something which adequately compensates for the liberties it has taken away?"

"I have the greatest admiration for what the Italians have done, though our methods will be different. I think their achievements adequately compensate for what they had before. I knew Italy before fascism, and it was in chaos."

"Do you believe that the Nazis can conceivably benefit Germany economically to an extent which would justify their cultural destructiveness?" was the next question.

"They have made a good beginning by reducing unemployment by 50 per cent in their first year," replied Sir Oswald; "while in Britain and the United States, both technically capable of a greater effort than Germany, unemployment has been reduced some 22 and 14 per cent, respectively."

"In your book you say that 'other and sterner measures' might be necessary to save the State in a situation 'approaching anarchy.' You would not use violence against the forces of the Crown but 'only against the forces of anarchy if and when the machinery of the State had been allowed to drift into powerlessness.' Who would be the judge of the powerlessness of the State, of whether the time had come to use violence 'against the forces of anarchy'?"

"The definition of such a situation is: when a government fails to preserve order, when 'the writ of government ceases to run' and the State is in anarchy."

"It is said by some that the Conservative party thinks of adopting the Blackshirts, much as the German Nationalists vainly sought to adopt and control the Nazis. Is this so?"

"We have no relations of any kind with the Conservative party," answered Sir Oswald. "We are equally opposed to conservatism and socialism and draw membership about equally from both parties. At York the other day I said that fascism was 'a revolution of the national spirit which was something very different from a Tory tea party or a Socialist mothers' meeting.' We shall not compromise but shall continue independently."

When asked about the attitude of British fascism to women, Sir Oswald replied: "We stand by the British tradition in regard to women and shall honor and elevate them in the State. Women hold high places in our movement. An attitude to women which is essentially racial must not be confused with fascism."

Thus, as expounded by Sir Oswald, British fascism advocates the corporative State in place of the political State, but expects— or at least hopes—that it can be brought about without such violence or intimidation as accompanied the rise of fascism in Italy and Germany. But this depends, he says, upon how bad the state of the nation becomes. Communists would be suppressed—so far as any could be found in Britain—and some degree of freedom (to be decided according to the severity of the crisis) would be permitted.

No Longer an Isle, Britain Moves Uncertainly

by D. W. Brogan

ON A summer Sunday evening of last year the inhabitants of Somerset were startled by the sight, low overhead, of the Hindenburg back from New York. It flew low; one could read the name and see the swastika without any difficulty; it was a superb sight, a magnificent demonstration of German craftsmanship—and a great German mistake. For it evoked memories all over England of the days when Zeppelins came on warlike errands; it reminded the man in the street (and still more the woman in the home) of what he and she would like to forget—that Britain is no longer an island.

And when the Basque city of Guernica was bombed there was genuine and abundant moral indignation in England; there was also resentment at the fresh realization that this old inviolate island was no better off and might well be worse off than her Continental neighbors. Since those neighbors have long been used to the painful idea of invasion by land, the shock of the new methods of war is far less felt in French public opinion than in British. And that irritation and bewilderment extends from the governed to the governors and back again; the governed affected by skepticism of

From the *New York Times Magazine,* July 4, 1937, copyright © 1937, 1965 by The New York Times Company.

the skill and resolution of the governor, and the governors nervous (not without reason) of the degree to which they can count on the support of the nation in any determined policy that may involve the risk of war. For in war (unlike cricket or football) it is a disadvantage to have to play at home—and Britain will have to play at home in the future as she has not had to do since the Middle Ages.

Can we wonder, then, that British policy seems uncertain, timid, inconsistent; that the government gives the impression of a nervous duelist, warning his opponent not to provoke him beyond the boundaries of endurance, and yet revealing that the last boundaries of endurance are not merely remote but elastic?

The mass of the British people accepts this prudence with an unusual calm. It may regret the necessity of the caution, but it does not deny its existence; and any government that forgets the great changes in Britain's position that now so deeply influence British policy will have a short lease of life.

Britain is no longer an island, and the British people are painfully adapting themselves to a new psychology, to the psychology of a people which realizes that if there is war, it will not be fought abroad but in large part will take the form of making a hell of England's green and pleasant land.

It is not the sense of the necessity of making great sacrifices in war that appals the British people. It is the realization that the days are over of the old British way of war—sending small professional armies overseas, hiring comparatively cheap foreigners to eke out the small military resources of Britain and exercising what had come to be regarded as an automatic naval supremacy. The late war was itself, in its conduct, a painful novelty. It was necessary (or thought necessary) to raise great armies like those of France and Germany; the whole population was directly or indirectly enrolled in war work. English social institutions like the Derby, fox hunting, professional football were seriously interfered with.

Like her Continental Allies, England was in a state of siege; less intense than that of France or Germany, but rigorous to a degree unknown in previous British history. It has often been pointed out since 1914 that Jane Austen (who belonged to a naval family) has hardly an indication in her novels that her young men are courting and sulking while the Corsican Ogre is menacing the liberties of Europe. Except for the mild comic relief of the amours of the militia officers or slight references to the navy, the great war (as its contemporaries called it) left only the most superficial traces on the work of so acute a social observer.

As far as the work of the greatest of English women novelists goes, the "testament of youth" of the generation of Napoleon is that agreeable young women, if they keep their heads, will get their men, for young men are there to be got. A hundred years later the young men were only available in brief periods snatched from constant menace of death and mutilation. The memory of that war, with its intrusions on liberty and life, with conscription and bread cards, with death entering hundreds of thousands of homes, with the memory of those long days when the noise of the guns in Flanders tormented so many households in Southern England, is, in itself, enough to account for the reluctance of any British Government to appear belligerent.

But there is more; there are memories of nights and even of days when the guns were firing not in Flanders but in London; when women and children shivered or stifled in the subways or cellars waiting for the "all clear," and when the great city knew (for the first time since the Dutch sailed up the Thames in 1667) what it was to have an enemy at the gates. Four times in a century Parisians had known what that meant; but the capital of the empire on which the sun never sets no more expected such an ordeal than did the Romans of Trajan's or Hadrian's time foresee the barbarian menace that would in a generation or two surround the Eternal City with walls.

The air raids of the late war were more important as an augury of future menace than as a threat to British security. They were irritating but not deadly. Far more serious at the time was the submarine blockade. Britain "commanded the seas" as was her custom and, in the mind of the man in the street, her right. The man in the street may have been deeply disappointed by the comparatively inglorious result of the Battle of Jutland, but the substantial results of the battle were those that the royal navy had accustomed its employers to expect. England would not be invaded; Germany would be held tight in the vise of blockade.

Yet within a year it was very doubtful if the British Government would be able to resist much longer. There was imminent danger that the close-packed millions on the little island, joined by trade and tradition to all corners of the world, would be cut off, starved into surrender as the Germans had starved Paris in 1871; as Britain was attempting to starve Germany in 1917. Both dangers were conjured away, but they remain, and their memory remains. And it is right that the memory should remain and remain acute. For the airplane and the submarine have transformed the character of British participation in war and, as befits a practical people, the attitude of the nation toward war.

The historical picture of the past accepted by the average man and woman in Britain was of wars in which games were often lost by folly but redeemed by gallantry and by the invariable rule of nature that the rubber was won by the nation that held the sea. Britain was that nation. Against that truth Napoleon had struggled in vain. War was no light matter, but it was its course and cost that had to be worried about—not its outcome. Britain could afford to "muddle through" because she was immune to dangerous if not to flesh wounds. Those days are over and the public in a vague but deep fashion knows it and the rulers of Britain know that they know it.

It is not only that "muddling through" no longer seems a tolerable way of conducting war now that there is no certainty that Britain will get time to muddle successfully. Muddling seems to acquire a less amusing aspect when it brings death on the scale of the last war. The British public has seldom admired its generals for their intellectual merits. They have been, in the popular mind, bluff fellows who got British troops into positions when the well-known inability of the British grenadier to know when he was beaten did the rest.

It was possible to believe that Waterloo was won on the playing fields of Eton. Or if that was difficult, it was possible to smile kindly at the idea. It was possible to share Kipling's scorn for those unfortunate Continental armies whose officers went to the front in trains, a detestable modern trick not taught at the school which produced "Stalky and Company."

But when the casualties of the first and barren day of the Battle of the Somme totaled 60,000, a good deal more than the number of all British troops engaged at Waterloo, the "old school tie" seemed less of an emblem of inevitable victory than it had in 1914. The Germans and French, whose officers went to the front in trains, seemed to do about as well as the British, whose leaders rode to the front on such nice shiny horses. The playing fields of Eton or of Clifton seemed a poor training for the mud bath of Passchendaele (the wilderness of British military history) when they did not even train a general like Haig to do what any good cricket captain learns to do—refuse to play on a soaking-wet wicket.

Nor was this disillusionment confined to the government, which had as full information on the point as military trade-union spirit would allow. We know from Mr. Lloyd George's memoirs how deep was his skepticism of the competence of the British military mind and machine. But the skepticism spread far wider than the War Cabinet. It spread by word of mouth from soldiers on leave, from soldier to soldier, each arguing that his show had been the greatest and most sanguinary mess of the year.

For the first time in British history, millions of men learned what the army mind was like at close quarters, and their reports home had something of the awe of an explorer who has just found a whole tribe of dinosaurs defying science by flourishing in the twentieth century. The British soldier, like the British man in the street, is too good tempered to bear malice, but he is not such a fool as he sometimes looks; he knew that there had been muddling on a vast scale and the heirs of the unbeatable soldiery of Wellington (who themselves did not hesitate to criticize the Duke) if they still did not know when they were beaten, did know when they had not won. Passchendaele might be a victory in Haig's dispatches or in his official life, but it was no victory in the eyes of the survivors who called themselves the "P. B. I."—the "Poor Bloody Infantry."

Memories of the late war, fears of the next war—these combine to make the British public highly skeptical of any policy that seems to risk involvement in a war of the old type run in the old way, with the addition of all the changes for the worse in Britain's position that were revealed between 1914 and 1918. It is natural, then, that pacifism in some form or other should be a political force that any government has to face, a political force hardly less formidable than the isolationism of the Middle West in the United States. Some of that pacifism, like Aldous Huxley's, is complete; given his premises, complete pacifism is logical and desirable. But, though the unconditional peace pledge is being widely signed, it is not and will not be of great political importance. A British Government will have more conscientious objectors on its hands in the next war, but that is all.

Nor is the pacifism of the famous Oxford resolution much more important. The purpose and character of the Oxford Union resolution not to "fight for King and country" was widely misunderstood. It was not a refusal to fight but a refusal to fight blindly, automatically, in obedience to the atavistic appeal of the two emotion-breeding words, "King and country." Many thousands of young men (most of them not connected with any of the universities that followed the Oxford lead) will refuse to volunteer for a war that seems simply an old imperialist war over again.

It will, no doubt, be possible to disguise the character of the war. But for this group the place of Russia will probably be decisive. Russia's participation will not automatically sanctify a war, but if Britain enters a combination against Russia the pacifists of the Oxford school will take a lot of convincing that this is not the old "King and country" story over again. There are, of course, other groups which would probably refuse to fight on the same side as Soviet Russia, but all together these political and ethical pacifists are not numerous or representative enough to worry this or any other British Government.

What is worrying the government is an unreflective tortoise-like pacifism. It is only verbally paradoxical to say that the realization that Britain is no longer an island has made millions cling to the insular idea. Realizing that a centuries-old immunity is over, the average man and, still more, the average woman (and more than half the voters are women) is, at times, ready to listen to any siren voices that can persuade him or her that Britain is "not a part of Europe," that it is open to a British government to imitate America or Canada—turn away from the Continent and join an immune and happy group of English-speaking peoples.

As fearful as any Middle Western Senator of foreign guile and entanglements, this numerous group of voters, and the writers and politicians who cater to their illusions, believe that Britain will be betrayed by any Continental allies that she may have, that she has nothing to lose or gain in Europe, and that, by refusing to touch the accursed thing, she can remain clean and safe. This spirit lay behind the general indifference to the German breach of Locarno by the occupation of the Rhineland. Arguments based on the necessity of honoring the national signature meant nothing to this class of persons and that any such question should have been raised added to the irritation felt against the French.

Anti-French feeling is undoubtedly strong in this group, but its base is less dislike of the French for doing what they do than for being where they are. If they were not so near, if there were not awkward traditions and engagements to defend French territory, it would be possible, so it is felt, to keep out of Continental wars altogether. And if the French would only behave themselves (that is, think first of British interests instead of their own selfish designs), the regrettable fact that the Channel is only twenty miles across and not getting any wider could be tolerated. But the French, with their alliances and doctrines of "an indivisible peace," are involving themselves in a net from which war is the only issue. Why should not Britain invoke a plague on both your houses and leave France and Germany and Russia and Italy to their doom?

"Why not?" is the answer of multitudes and of individuals of some importance. Let Germany make war on Russia, swallow Czechoslovakia; what business is it of Britain's? If the war can be kept east of the Rhine, why worry? This indifference to the balance of power and to the effect on Britain's imperial position after a war in which, whether a participant or not, Japan must be a winner or loser, illustrates the bewilderment of the public mind.

For the preachers of this view are not, in the main, the old-fashioned radical pacifists but self-styled imperial realists. No one has opened Lord Palmerston's grave, but he must have been tossing badly during the last few years!

This policy, though widely accepted and preached in high places, has little chance of adoption. The rulers of Britain are practical men, and they know that isolation was never less feasible than now—unless the price is paid; and that price is a surrender of the imperial position of Britain. No more than in 1914, can Britain let France be destroyed, and so Britain is tied to French policy; she can warn, she can attempt to bully, but in the long run, for geographical and military, as well as for economic and imperial reasons, Britain and France, the two western empires that hold so much that other people want, have to stick together. That sticking together may be disguised under phrases like "our common democratic ideals" but the basis of this unwilling union is factual, not ideal. If there is a war, Britain will be in it and on the French side. Editors may pontificate and German diplomats give parties, but the decision is inevitable.

There remains, however, a realist group which admits these facts but which hopes to return to the "old British way" of waging war. Mackenzie King recently expressed his belief that not only would Canada never send an army overseas again but that Britain would not. Memories of a dreadful military effort have led many persons (for example, the most influential British military critic, Liddell Hart) to argue that Britain should decide for herself in the next war what share she will take. She is not, it is argued, to be tied to French military methods, not to send millions of men to France; she is to go back to the good old days of limited-liability wars, to the age of Jane Austen. This is a subtler type of wishful thinking—but it is wishful thinking all the same.

Britain is menaced not with inconvenience but with death if the Channel ports fall into hostile hands and she will have to fight as hard as she knows how. In the good old days a British general like Wellington manoeuvring in a foreign country could display admirable fortitude when it came to sacrificing his ally's territory. He could always sail home if need be and in general act like the

Irish landlord who wrote from London that if his tenants thought they could intimidate him by shooting his bailiff they were much mistaken.

But, as Mr. Baldwin has pointed out, Britain's frontier is now on the Rhine; and, as Lord Haig said in 1918, the British Army (just like those of the Continent) may find itself with its back to the wall. This, too, the government, it may be suspected, realizes, and this unpleasant truth the nation suspects. The days of limited-liability wars, like the days of British immunity from complete defeat, are over.

No one can doubt that the British people, the most patriotic in the world, will readjust itself to its worsened position. But the readjustment will take time. And, while it is going on, politicians will play safe and show no morbid fear of backing down. It is not a dignified policy but it has much to recommend it, for a country whose rulers remember that the real lesson of the late war was that the internal unity of a nation was a surer guarantee of victory than a first-class military machine. That unity does not exist at the moment in Britain and its creation is as anxiously awaited by the British Government as is the completion of any number of warships.

British foreign policy is bound to be that of a formerly very rich man slowly learning to live within comparatively straitened means. Such a man will get used to it in time, but at the beginning he is liable to excessive penury. In British foreign policy that penury is reflected in a willingness to swallow affronts—an attitude that can be made to seem ridiculous but may be, for the moment, wise. At any rate the British elector is unwilling to take any risks that can be avoided and the politician (even when he doubts the wisdom of this course) will obey orders, hoping that time will restore to Britain some of that self-confidence that she owned yesterday—as no doubt time will.

Grimly Britain Tackles a Grim Task

by Sir Philip Gibbs

LONDON

A FEW evenings ago when I waited outside the German Embassy, where many cars and luggage vans stood ready to take its staff to the train, I remembered an incident of twenty-five years ago which brought back in a flash vivid memories of the first days of the war in 1914. Twenty-five years ago I saw the secretary of the German Embassy lock the door of the Chancellery on the first day of the war with England, and on this evening, a quarter of a century later, my mind jerked back to the mood and spirit of England then.

It was a different England. It was a different mood. We knew nothing of modern warfare between great powers with immense machinery of slaughter. Our previous wars had not revealed the terrific concentration of gun power. War in the air was still unknown.

In 1914 the declaration of war following the German invasion of Belgium had not been preceded by long negotiations and warnings. It came from the blue like a thunderbolt. Three weeks previously the English people were still playing tennis on their lawns and boating on their rivers without a thought that they might become involved in a life and death struggle. When it came, after Sarajevo and Germany's invasion of Belgium, England was unprepared except at sea and everything had to be improvised.

The call for volunteers—the first 100,000—by Lord Kitchener was answered by a rush of youth to the recruiting booths. Most of these young men went eagerly from schools, universities, factories and fields. It seemed to them a great adventure. They hated the idea of missing it. They were anxious lest they might be too late to go out to France before Christmas, when it would be over, as most believed.

I remember seeing battalions of these boys marching through London, cheering wildly outside Buckingham Palace. Everywhere on the first night of the war crowds sang "God Save the King" and other patriotic songs. Only the fathers and mothers were sad and anxious. The youth of those days were light-hearted for the most part about the coming struggle. In camps and on the roads they sang music-hall songs with great gusto.

One remembers those old refrains: "Pack up your troubles in your old kit bag," "Hullo, hullo, it's a different girl again." One ditty of no great merit—"It's a Long, Long Way to Tipperary"—became the marching song of all these young troops, and afterward in France and Flanders it almost became our national anthem, though it had no meaning.

I have heard none of these songs or any others during the past two days. England's mood now is different and grimmer.

There was a lot of flag-wagging in 1914. Union Jacks fluttered everywhere, and England's children waved them and cheered in slum streets and London parks.

No flags were carried by those masses of children who were evacuated from London and other great cities during recent days.

There were still hansom cabs in London on declaration of war in 1914. Young bloods rode on top of them, laughing and cheering. Restaurants were crowded until dawn. Theatres were packed. "Chu-Chin Chow" was the most popular show. In London and other cities there was a kind of feverish gayety, and our old spirit of adventure in England, our old fighting tradition, our exultation of youth called upon for service in time of danger were not appalled by a horrifying vision of those Four Horsemen who were riding over Europe.

Young girls soon began to appear in the streets in strange uniforms. Women soon began to take men's places with laughing cheerfulness. It was the war which first broke down the Victorian tradition of women's place being in the home and of a sheltered life which not even the suffragettes had overthrown.

As I look back on 1914 it seems to me now that the war in its early days was greeted by the mass of English folk as a great liberation and a most exciting change, taking them away from drudgery, solitude, boredom and triviality to this new adventure which they thought would be a short, dramatic, heroic episode.

There were, of course, more serious minds. More spiritual motives. Young men like Rupert Brooke went with a crusader's spirit to fight for England in her hour of need, to fight for liberty, to rescue life's beauty from an ugly militarism. They were willing to offer their lives for this noble cause. They were uplifted by the finest sense of patriotism because of their deep love of all that was best in England and Scotland.

Those first legions of youth who had been quick to volunteer were the fine flower of the land and a splendid crowd. But they knew nothing of the barrage of fire and the high-explosive shell. They knew nothing of poison gas. They knew nothing of aerial bombardment. They knew very little, one must admit, about the causes of that war in 1914.

It is all different now. England is different. Its mood is different. We are a people well informed about the cause of this war and about its powers of evil and destruction.

The wireless has made an immense difference to public thought. In almost every little home during this long period of international tension, and through these constant crises, the radio has brought daily news information which has enabled humble folk in all social classes to know as much as the diplomats and statesmen. Farmers, cottagers, factory hands, assistant clerks—all kinds of workers by hand and brain have been able to follow every move on the international chessboard in a way which was utterly beyond their reach a quarter of a century ago. They have been able to form their own judgment with that shrewd conviction which generally gets to the essential truth of things. There is no doubt what that judgment is today. The man in the street, the man in the third-class carriage, the factory hand and the mechanic, the field laborer and the small farmer have made up their minds that Hitler must be put out, even at the expense of a war which they know will be costly.

They hate war. England was the most peace-loving country in Europe. But these people, as far as I know them, believe in their souls that life had become intolerable while Hitler went on threatening the peace of Europe and the liberties of all nations.

They don't put it that way. They say: "We are fed up with that man. We've no quarrel with the German people and we're sorry for them, but we're fed up with this Nazi business and all it means. It's got to be killed." That is the verdict of the common man who is risking his life to see the sentence carried out. It is the verdict, roughly put, of the whole British nation, who backed Prime Minister Chamberlain's policy of appeasement until Hitler broke all his pledges and betrayed even his own hatreds and passions, which he called his creed, by his pact with Russia, whom he had shriekingly denounced for six years as the arch-enemy of mankind.

But there is none of the light-heartedness of 1914. The marching youth is not singing gay old songs. There is no flag-wagging, cheering or sense of adventure that may be more amusing than the drudgery of daily life. The adventure has gone out of war. What price glory? as someone asked.

The British mood is stern, grim, serious. We know now all there is to know about war. On village greens in England, Scotland and Wales stand memorials to the fathers of sons who are now called up for service. A million of them. Fathers and mothers of lads now in the ranks of the militia and all services went through the last war and remember it with all its agonies, all its darkness. They have no illusions.

This air menace has brought every home into the front line. No one is safe. No child, even, is safe. The whole population of

the British Isles is in the war zone. We look up into the blue
sky of these September days and wonder when they are coming.
Every man and woman has a gas mask slung across the shoulders
or carried in a vanity bag. Tonight or tomorrow a foul breath
may creep down London streets. Incendiary bombs may fall,
making London a city of flame.

The long preparations for war, which a thousand times was
said not to be inevitable, prepared the British mind for what
might come. The crisis of September a year ago, when we stood
on the edge of a dark pit two and a half hours away from its
furnace fires, was a terrifying shock which awoke the nation to
grim reality. In 1914 Britain was unprepared. In 1939 on the
first day of the war it was prepared in its soul and its national
organization for defense.

The evacuation from London and other great cities was carried out, as all the world knows, without a hitch. From London
alone went more than 600,000 children, called from their homes
by a Pied Piper who sent a whisper over many wires. Everything
was ready for them, and it was certainly a marvelous demonstration not only of efficient organization but of the charity and kind-
liness of all British folk who have filled their own houses with
these little refugees, abandoning their own comfort to make these
little ones happy.

London, the capital of a great empire, now looks very deserted
and forlorn without its child life. I drove through many of its
streets and they were empty of traffic and crowds. It was like a
besieged city. Up above glittered hundreds of kite balloons,
silver in the blue sky as once I saw them, though not so many,
above our lines in France and Flanders. Newly recruited policemen in steel helmets stood under archways. Sentries outside the
Palace and Marlborough House had steel shelters for sentry
boxes.

How different now from that London of 1914, with its excited,
cheering crowds, its crowded restaurants, its fleets of hansom
cabs klop-klopping down Piccadilly and Pall Mall!

But there is only one thing, really, which matters. Is the spirit
of British youth the same? Have they the courage of their fathers?
Will they go through this war, with its infernal ordeal, calling

for desperate will power with the same dogged courage and resolution as those who fought from 1914 onward?

There were people who did not think so. The Germans were told in every lecture, every book, every newspaper that the youth of Britain were decadent and effete, that they had lost their traditions and the will to defend their national heritage.

That has been proved already to have been a monstrous slander. As soon as recruiting started for the navy, army, air service and militia it was seen that these young recruits were of fine physique and first-class quality. There had been a lot of talk about the poor physical state of many boys, but these lads startled recruiting officers with their high standard. More encouraging even than that is their fine standard of intelligence and character. A naval officer at Portsmouth, in charge of naval recruits, told me that he was embarrassed by their ability.

"They are all fit to be officers," he told me. "Discipline is easy because they discipline themselves. One has only to show them what to do once or twice and they do it like experienced hands. They have technical instinct and are so keen on their jobs that they learn very rapidly."

The same verdict is given about the young men of the Royal Air Force who have already singed their wings over Germany and had their baptism of fire.

Looking at them here and there, I feel that the hands of the clock have been put back a quarter century. These boys are exactly like their fathers whom I used to meet on the roads of France or in Flemish airdromes. They have the same look in their eyes, the same spirit behind that look, the same quality of character. All is right with British youth, not only in the British Isles themselves but in all the dominions of our commonwealth of nations.

I thought I knew England. It has been my study for books and articles. As an Englishman living in country districts more than in London, I thought I knew that those fellows playing cricket on the village green, refusing to be scared by the crisis, laughing at the name of Hitler as though at a good joke, would not be found wanting when the call came for them—though I prayed God it would never come and had more faith than was justified in human sanity over there in Germany. But now I am staggered a little by the quiet courage revealed during recent days.

There has been no panic. There has been no hysteria. There has been no boasting. The British people have faced this thing with astonishing resolution, calm and grim resignation, though they know it will be very frightful.

It would be absurd to pretend that none of them is afraid. Shell fire is not amusing. Death is not a joke, especially if it comes to one's women and children. There is fear at the back of many minds—but not enough to weaken resolution, not enough to overbalance that courage which faces everything and carries on.

So it was in the last war. So it is now.

Part 2

YEARS OF HEROISM, 1939–1951

ONLY IN the summer of 1940 did the British people experience the scourge of war at first hand, as the *Luftwaffe,* in a preliminary to a German invasion, hurled tons of bombs from the sky at Britain's urban centers. Beneath the protective shield of the RAF, strained to its limits, the populace shared with those heroic pilots England's finest hour. Not only did they walk, work, and sleep with the menace of death, but they were also subjected to all sorts of harassment in the disruption of their routines. The correspondents of the *New York Times* shared those frustrations, as Raymond Daniell's account graphically illustrates. The Battle of Britain was sooner won than anyone realized; though the misnamed "Blitz" continued well into 1941, Hitler began to disengage his forces in mid-September 1940—the Nazis' proposed invasion was postponed, then canceled, for the winter. For the first time the civilian population's ability to endure sustained air attacks had been established. Unfortunately, allied leaders did not learn the lesson. Strategic—read, terror—bombing proved as inefficacious when subsequently directed against

Germany and Japan: the home fronts held up throughout the war.

And yet the domestic scene in Britain, under the intense pressure of war, altered considerably. Early in the war James Reston observed a heightened social consciousness, with widespread ramifications for the fabric of national life. Where Daniell had claimed that "the pressure is never off . . . it is almost impossible to live a normal life or think normal thoughts," Reston judged to the contrary that "one good thing about this modern war is that it is giving people time to think." Implicit in this observation was the recognition that governments could, and ought to, take the lead in planning solutions to the nation's social and economic grievances. Further, Labour's leaders were now well placed to implement change, since they had accepted office under Churchill in May 1940. Reston surely is correct in viewing total war as an agent of domestic change.

Politicians and civil servants alike strove to plan measures of reconstruction, in order to avoid the deep disappointment and disillusionment which had followed the First World War. Though some progress was made in wartime—town and country planning, in part a response to damage inflicted by German bombs, and the Education Act of 1944—the implementation of the Beveridge Report was deferred until the war's end. In fact, the Labour government of 1945 not only established a comprehensive system of social security, including unemployment, medical, and old-age benefits, but also financed the Welfare State in a more radical fashion than even Beveridge had proposed. Yet there were those who would have scuttled such planning for reconstruction in favor of a return to the shibboleths of the inter-war years. Such antediluvian attitudes were satirically scorned by David Low, the finest political cartoonist of the day. In conducting an interview with his favorite subject, the well-known Colonel Blimp, Low warned against a return to the untrammeled system of private enterprise. But better to permit Colonel Blimp to speak for himself.

That the war was meanwhile won must be credited in large part to Winston Churchill, whom Isaiah Berlin has aptly described as "saviour of his country." Whatever criticisms may be directed aaginst Churchill's administration, his supreme contribution to victory must not be forgotten. Churchill, however, was not an easy man to work with. As his personal chief of staff, General Ismay, once remarked, "When things are going well, he is good; when things are going badly, he is superb; but when things are going half-well, he is 'hell on wheels.' " Some of Churchill's military advisers resented his continuous interference in strategic matters; and in some judgments they simply thought him incorrect. Though Drew Middleton's account of Churchill as war strategist is dated 1958, the criticisms of Churchill's judgment, recorded by those working with him, were made during the war. But none of his critics would deny Churchill his heroic stature.

Nor did the need for heroism cease with victory in Europe and the Far East: a quieter kind of fortitude—a stoic endurance —was required to accept the rigors of postwar austerity. A longtime European correspondent, Anne O'Hare McCormick, sketched Britain's somber national mood, the product of economic dislocation in the aftermath of war. Most Englishmen had recognized the inevitability of austerity, even if they failed to share Sir Stafford Cripps's masochistic forbearance with the subject. Yet Mrs. McCormick rightly pointed out the dangers inherent in its prolongation. Economic realities, however, do not necessarily yield to patience and courage. Britain's postwar economy touched bottom in 1947—*Annus Horrendus* in the view of Hugh Dalton, the Chancellor of the Exchequer—but no recovery could restore the British economy to a position of world primacy. In economic terms, Great Britain had fought one war too many: Barbara Ward, Foreign Editor of *The Economist* in 1948, pointed out the need both for a dramatic expansion of British productivity and for the nation to assume leadership in creating a new economic pattern for western Europe. By 1970, British productivity had fallen behind continental standards, and the new Conservative government was, once again, negotiating the question of British membership in the conspicuously successful Common Market. The nation's postwar economic problems have proved of long duration.

Nor was all well with the Welfare State. A Liberal journalist associated with the *Manchester Guardian,* Richard Fry, maintained that the Welfare State had been carelessly erected. While his comments about the allegedly activist role of inter-war governments are misleading, Fry properly queried the stifling of individual incentive and the burden of taxation required to sustain the vast structure that was the Welfare State. Whether Britain's level of taxation remains unnecessarily high because of the sleight-of-hand involved in funding the Welfare State is in 1970 an open question: Tory electoral campaigning featured a promise of basic reform of the tax structure, and the first Budget presented by the new Conservative government took an initial step in that direction.

Surely the Welfare State, a heroic feat of social planning in the midst of economic dislocation, will stand largely intact, including its once most contentious program, the National Health Service. Already in 1940 Reston had pointed out that with the acceleration of social change, "most doctors here now believe that they will be working for the State at the end of the war." In fact, Attlee's government required more time, and the revolution in health care took effect only in 1948. Within a short time, objective observers regarded NHS as a success, as Herbert Matthews reported early in 1949. Since that time, several informative *New York Times* articles (Clifton Daniel, "A British Doctor Weighs the Health Service," July 5, 1953: Kenneth Robinson, "The Case for Britain's Health Service," November 18, 1962) have confirmed its success. Its costs, however, have consistently exceeded expectation, and the network of health centers foreseen by its founders has never been built. Though Labour and Conservative governments alike have introduced nominal charges for certain items under the program, the likelihood that any government would impose a charge for medical attention appears remote. The National Health Service remains a model other countries would do well to emulate.

When Total War Blasts a City

by Raymond Daniell

LONDON

CIVILIANS young and old are the real defenders of London. Upon their courage and endurance may depend the outcome of the Battle of Britain. This is total war in its most brutal and cruel form. None save those who have lived here, sharing the troubles of the people of this stricken capital since the Blitzkrieg started, can understand what they have been through, and none who has been here will ever forget their cheerfulness and calm throughout a crisis in their history.

Day in and day out all around the clock, London's millions have lived under the shadow of sudden death. For them there has been no safe and sure shelter, no possibility of retreat, no thought of surrender. Their only other choice was to stand and take it, and they have done so.

Thousands of homes, rich and poor, and even the palace where the King and Queen reside, have been bombed by ruthless raiders flying high and hurling destruction as carelessly as boys tossing pebbles into a well. Tons of dynamite have rained down on churches, hospitals and even crowded shelters. Not even the dead can rest in peace, for cemeteries have been torn up by blasting bombs. Blocks of houses have been leveled.

Only a small proportion of homes wrecked by Marshal Hermann Goering's raiders lies near military objectives, any more than Buckingham Palace, which is surrounded by parklike lawns with spreading trees and beds of flowers. The streets of Central London as well as the city's outlying sections have been torn up and deep craters show where bombs have landed. Tops of modern office buildings have been blown off and thousands of houses look out on the world through bleak-looking broken windows. The number of homeless refugees increases every day.

But these are major tragedies confined to relatively few of the 8,000,000 inhabitants; and they are easier to bear than the wear and tear of constant petty disturbances, dislocations and inconveniences that seem to accumulate as days and nights of hell on earth continue with less and less surcease from the presence of those agents of death swarming in from across the Channel.

It isn't as if every one could adopt a completely fatalistic attitude and go about ordinary tasks in the ordinary way. Modern urban life is too complicated for that. For instance, often during raid warnings gas pressure is reduced. The housewife preparing dinner for her breadwinner finds the fuel supply running low. Hours after the all-clear has sounded the husband, who has waited in a shelter until the raid ended, comes home late, tired, cross and jumpy. She tries to heat up the dinner but the siren wails again and the meal is served cold. The weary, nerve-racked people then face the problem of getting some sleep despite the threatening whine overhead interspersed with the bursting of bombs, the bark of anti-aircraft guns and the spatter of shrapnel and machine-gun bullets on the roof and against the windows.

If the family lives in their own house they have their own shelter only partly underground and far from immune to a direct hit or even a very close one. To such a shelter, with tea kettle and alcohol lamp, thousands of families repair at nightfall to spend the night on folding cots, waiting for daybreak—another day of what Prime Minister Churchill aptly described as "blood, toil, tears and sweat."

Nearly every one in London has taken up shelter life in

earnest now. One result the Blitzkrieg has had has been to deplete the stocks in London shops of such articles as folding cots, mattresses, sleeping bags, vacuum bottles and other things Londoners formerly associated with holidays and fun but that now have become a grimly necessary part of their lives.

Residents of the poor East End can be seen on a nightly tragic hegira westward in search of what they regard as better shelters, further away from their own quarter, which in the early days bore the brunt of the attack from the skies. They are a weary and bedraggled horde, carrying their blankets and clutching cheap, battered old suitcases.

Smart hotels present a different picture. All of them have exerted great efforts and spared no expense to make their shelters attractive. In one which has a grill room deep underground dancing goes on nightly until after midnight. As soon as the orchestra folds up its instruments the scene changes. In marches a flock of guests, some dressed, some wearing dressing gowns or negligees, all carrying sleeping bags or quilts or cushions which they spread upon the floor and settle down for the night.

At the beginning one could look forward to the day with little fear of serious interruption. Goering's daylight raids after the first maulings the Luftwaffe suffered at the hands of the R. A. F. usually came at fairly regular times and were confined chiefly to reconnaissance flights to see what damage had been done on the night before and light new fires to guide the coming night's raiders on their murderous mission. Now it is getting so that there are fewer and shorter intervals between alarms and one has to decide whether to live permanently underground or try to get about one's business in the city with its traffic snarls and always with the prospect of being buried under falling masonry or smashed to bits by a bursting bomb.

A funny thing about the raids is the effect they have upon one's imagination and one's ears. After nearly a fortnight of it one awaits and anticipates the sound of the sirens as a patient shrinks from the dentist's drill. The pressure is never off; try as one will, it is almost impossible to live a normal life or think normal thoughts. And the worst of it is that there is no end in sight.

Thus far the nation has been able to maintain its principal

lines of communication, both internal and external, and industrial production has not dropped sharply, as the Germans probably hoped it would. That is especially true of the industries turning out planes and weapons for Britain's defense. But night and day raids have had a paralyzing effect on London's shops and entertainment and normal workaday life.

The theatres are all closed and every time the sirens sound the big shops pull down their shutters and show their customers to basement shelters. No one wants to move far from home, because there is no telling how one will get back. Taxicab drivers are sometimes willing to risk short daylight sprints, but after dark London is like a deserted city, with hardly a pedestrian in sight.

The problem of telling American newspaper readers about what is happening here is turning the correspondents' hair gray. Since the indiscriminate bombing started the London staff of this newspaper has been doing most of its writing in a cellar filled with gesticulating Frenchmen, shouting, scampering messengers and a constant procession of tired and hungry office workers trapped by a raid while they were homeward bound.

Space and telephone facilities are limited in this cellar and it is necessary to funnel all the thousands of words sent out from here each night over a single telephone wire to the cable office, where the dispatches are read by censors and, one hopes, soon afterward transmitted. If they are not, it may be hours before that fact is known. But there are few messengers willing to risk their necks in a hail of shrapnel and bursting bombs.

But this is war, and one cannot complain. The security and future freedom of this nation and the welfare of the United States depend upon the outcome of this struggle, and whether the fight is won or lost will depend not only upon armies and soldiers, but upon men wearing the uniforms of firemen, policemen, air-raid wardens, demolition squads, first-aid corps and upon the efficiency and bravery of men and women wearing no uniforms at all, but repairing damaged water mains, gas pipes, telephone lines and railroad tracks under fire.

For the outcome of this battle depends upon maintenance of the people's morale; and, dogged as is British character and tough the fibre of a Briton's soul, a breakdown in essential services of this great city would be Hitler's strongest ally. In the opening stages of the battle these unsung heroes of London's defense have shown their mettle.

Night after night this correspondent has seen them calmly putting out fires, rescuing the injured, repairing damage while debris was still falling about them.

It takes as much heroism to dig out a 1,000-pound delayed-action bomb near the foundations of St. Paul's as it does to hold an outpost in the face of a tank charge and that is the kind of heroism with which the people of this city are defending their homes and hearths. And they are keeping their sense of humor, managing to laugh and joke through it all. They may be beaten, but they will be the last to know it.

Social Upheaval in Britain

by James Reston

LONDON

THERE IS a great stirring of social consciousness among the people of Great Britain. To its very foundations their society has been jarred by German bombs. Many old habits, traditions and prejudices have been broken down; many false values have been smashed. There is a new, positive spirit of reconstruction in the air which, born of necessity, sorrow and death, may be a deceptive, passing phase; but, at least for the time being, the British people are thinking new thoughts and dreaming brave dreams.

This new spirit was negative at first. A generation that had gone through one war was cynical about a second war which they felt could have been avoided. The "nothing's good" school was pretty cynical early in the war and there was a good deal of bickering between the left and right, but this has died down to a certain extent now and the spirit of all classes is much more positive.

The bombing of thousands of slum dwellings, the introduction of new men and methods and techniques in government industry, the evacuation of hundreds of thousands of people from urban to rural communities have all led to a more constructive questioning about the foundations of our modern society. The people see that when the war is over they are going to have to start all over again and rebuild not only houses, factories and roads that have been smashed but establish an economic, financial and social system that won't break down again. One good thing about this modern war is that it is giving people time to think about these things.

The evacuation of children, the rationing of gasoline and night-long air raids have all led to a much more simple and thoughtful way of life. All the "time-killers" of modern society—movies, night clubs, dinner parties—have been drastically curtailed. People have gone back to the habits of the eighteenth century. They are reading more, thinking more; the loss of their friends and possessions and the hourly fear of sudden death have made them more curious and introspective. They know only too well now that the action of politicians can affect their lives in the most devastating way, and thousands of them are watching these politicians closely and trying to figure out not only what happened to bring them into this war but what is happening to them and to the structure of their State at the present time.

They see, first of all, that war is speeding up the process of leveling down the classes—a process which has been going on slowly here ever since the end of the last war. This leveling is being accomplished by taxation, by government decree and by German bombs. Outside the war industries and export trade it is a downright liability to own business or property here now, because of the difficulty of getting raw materials, shipping and markets. Houses owned by the rich are lying empty, piling up taxes by the tens of thousands, and some of them are being bombed to the ground. Moreover, taxes on income are going up all the time and dividends are restricted.

The war at present is costing Britain about $40,000,000 a day. This country of 48,000,000 people is already burdened with a national debt of over $40,000,000,000 and will spend in the coming year about $14,000,000,000—half again as much as the highest budget ever presented to the 131,000,000 people of the United States—and the upper tenth of the population are now paying out up to nearly half their earnings to help meet their share.

Partly as the result of reduced earnings of the upper and middle classes, there are observed the beginnings of significant social change and education in this country. By an ingenious mixture of vocational and social training the "public schools" of Britain have trained rich men's sons for government services and professions ever since the beginnings of organized education here. These young men have not been "educated" so much as they have been taught a set of standardized attitudes toward life. They were taught how to rule and how to dress and speak. They were given a certain amount of discipline, and this system paid them well, because the men who had acquired the right attitudes got the good jobs.

Now, however, this system is cracking a little. First of all, the middle-class people of this country, who since the start of the present century have felt it necessary to make sacrifices in order to send their sons to these public schools, have been hit so hard by the war that they have had to bring the boys home. Even some upper-class people have not been able to afford $1,000 to send a 14-year-old boy to Eton for a year, and as a result some public schools are in financial difficulties. Already some fee schools have been doubled up and have reduced their fees. What is more, some boys evacuated from slums to villages near public schools have been more or less forced on some of these private schools by local authorities. That may not seem like much progress in New York, but over here it is a minor revolution.

Changes in the social structure are coming about in more violent ways, too. Take the case of doctors' hospitals in this country. Ever since the last war hospitals in Britain have struggled along on private charity. Throughout the Nineteen Thirties virtually every hospital in London was forced to advertise that it was so far in debt that it did not know what to do. The same thing has been true all over the country—large debts, dingy, run-down buildings, equipment that could not be compared with that of New York hospitals.

When the war broke out the government took over about 3,100 hospitals all over the country. Under the emergency hospital plan they enrolled 2,000 doctors in a free medical service for air-raid victims and paid them salaries ranging from $800 to $6,000 a year. They equipped 1,000 new operating rooms in existing hospitals and re-equipped a hundred dilapidated institutions. In other words, the government stepped in and did in eight months what would have taken at least eight years to do by voluntary contributions, and most doctors here now believe they will be working for the State at the end of the war.

As in health, so in housing is progress being made. Half a million children from the slums of London, Liverpool, Glasgow, Manchester, Birmingham and other cities have been evacuated to the country, where they are learning new ways of life, eating better, getting an education in communities where bombers are something of an exciting novelty rather than a nightly terror. There is not a sociologist in Britain who has not at some time or other pointed out the dangers of centralization, which has gone on here since the industrial revolution began. Authorities think the habits, health and morals of children will be better for dispersal, and they are convinced that evacuated children will contribute far more to the future of England than if they had stayed behind.

Even destruction, for all its evils, has given Britain a chance to rebuild. One of the few consolations about bombing is that the worst houses usually fall down in the greatest numbers. Prime Minister Churchill has appointed Sir John Reith to the job of planning to rebuild Britain, and Sir John has employed some of the finest architects in the country to help him. People whose houses have been destroyed or damaged in air raids have been guaranteed that the government will help them to rebuild after the war, and while many of the nation's noblest buildings can never be replaced, the housing of people will undoubtedly be better after the war.

The obvious question at this point is what guarantee has any one that these evidences of social progress will last? There is, of course, no guarantee, because nobody knows who is going to win this war, but certain political changes have taken place since the start of the war which may have a profound effect on the eventual social structure of the country.

When Mr. Churchill replaced the late Neville Chamberlain at 10 Downing Street the Labor party joined his government as a full partner. This party, which is socialist, has three seats in the war Cabinet and, through its control over industrial workers, it holds a strong veto power over almost anything Mr. Churchill wants to do. There is not the slightest suggestion of friction between Labor leaders and the Prime Minister, and there is not likely to be on most questions, but on the subject of the social reconstruction of this country this Labor element is already having a great deal to say, and it will have a lot more to say in the future.

For it is a mistake to think that this National Government of all the major political parties is just a temporary expedient. Win or draw, this nation at the end of this war is going to have more problems to solve than she has right now. The nation will need the cooperation of all parties. There are many reasons to believe that the age of shallow political bickerings is past here for a long time.

It is important, therefore, to look for a minute at the policy of this party. Ernest Bevin, who may replace Mr. Churchill, when and if that great man steps down, made a significant speech in London the other day. "I want to give you," he said, "a new motive for industry and for life. I suggest that at the end of this war and, indeed, during this war, we accept social security as a main motive of all our national life. That does not mean that all profits or surpluses would be wiped out, but it does mean that the whole of your economy, finance, organization, science, and everything, would be directed together to social security not for a small middle class or for those who may be merely possessors of property but for the community as a whole."

Speaking about unemployment after the war—which is the first social question that will have to be solved—Mr. Bevin said: "The greatest social implication arising out of this war is the effort to get rid of that horrible queue outside the labor exchanges. . . . I am afraid that unless the community is seized with the importance of this you may slip into revolutionary action. What I am horrified at is the thought of a blind revolution of starving men that is undirected and that ends in disaster for the whole community."

Mr. Bevin is not the only one worrying about this. Mr. Churchill is worrying about it and so are the Tories. In every discussion of social change in this country the first problem is what to do with 5,000,000 men now making munitions of war. All other social reforms, all new ideas, everything, including Britain's form of government, will be affected if not dominated by this consideration. In solving these problems of social and economic change Britain will probably compromise, as she has always compromised. For all the Socialists' talk of a brave new world she probably will not go socialist, and for all the fears of the Left she is not likely to go fascist in the strict definition of that term.

If she can keep from being defeated—and with American help she probably can do that—she will probably develop her own peculiar form of state capitalism. Long after the war is over finance, industry and even labor will probably be controlled by the government as they are now.

This government knows very well that the word dominating the minds of people all over Europe, the word that put Adolf Hitler into power and kept him there, was the word "security." For all the talk by British statesmen about "liberty," security is what these people want, too—even if they have to give up some liberty to get it.

The wealth of this country, as the Socialists desire, probably will be utilized to get that security. Railroads and factories probably will be nationalized. The old school tie monopoly in government services probably will be broken down.

All these things will probably happen, given freedom from Nazi domination, and time. As the nation rises from the evils of war, progress toward that secure, simple and equal life which most of these people really want will undoubtedly be made.

The popular fallacy at the moment is to believe, as so many people on the Left do, that war can cure all our social ills. As in the last war, when Ireland was set free and suffrage was extended, Britain will move forward. It is, however, but the start of the millennium. Utopia is not likely to rise out of purgatory.

Mr. Low Interviews Colonel Blimp

by David Low

BECAUSE Britain now has a smart up-to-date new army it has been said again that Colonel Blimp is dead. Such wild rumors could not rise except out of three misconceptions.

First, that he is an exclusively British phenomenon.

Second, that he is peculiar to the military profession.

Third, that he is mortal.

All these suppositions are incorrect.

Blimp is best identified as Stupidity—the stupidity of the fool who trips over his own confusion of thought. It is stupidity without race, nationality, party or creed. If I draw cartoons mostly about Blimp in Britain it is just because I happen to live there. There are Blimps in Russia, in China, all over Europe. (Let's ignore Germany and Japan.) Don't imagine you've not got plenty in America. When I hear some of the things American Blimps say—especially in answer to British Blimps—I often roll off my drawing board with sepulchral mirth.

No, Blimp is not dead. But he has Passed On, in the sense of moving to pastures new of post-war reconstruction and economics.

From the *New York Times Magazine,* April 2, 1944, copyright © 1944 by The New York Times Company.

In the old days the economic ideas of the British Blimp were conceived in a spirit of touching simplicity. He used to see himself as John Bull carrying in one hand a cricket bat, in the other the latest Trade Returns, being patted on the head by Britannia, who says with dignity, "Well done, Sir. England is proud of you." Over all the pound sterling is fixed shining in the sky.

From 1930 onward the picture was of himself with a stiff upper lip, chin up and back to the wall, standing alone (or perhaps with the Empire, which he sought to Draw Closer with the Crimson Bonds of Kinship, as though it were a bale of goods) seeking the Revival of Prosperity by Restoration of Confidence in something or other. . . . But a war like this one works changes.

Up till fairly recently Blimp resembled the famous old lady of the London blitz. Her house had been bombed, leaving only a jagged frontage sticking up in a flattened street, but she turned up in the morning as usual to scrub the doorstep from force of habit. Likewise Blimp, a little while ago. If you introduced the subject of post-war reconstruction he would pull out his doorstep and scrub away just as though the old national economic structure still stood behind it.

Time marches on. Today Blimp finds himself, somewhat glassy-eyed and red in the face, a sort of refugee among strange ideas in strange company under strange new slogans his understanding of which is frequently complicated not to say defeated by his old habits of thought. Instinctively he tries to wed ancient dogmas to new revelation much as a converted savage tries to combine cannibalism and Christianity.

"Cooperation and Collaboration among nations? Gad, Sir, yes, indeed. But no restriction of the sacred principle of Competition, every man for himself and the devil take the hindmost. Coordination of national policies for mutual prosperity? Gad, Sir, by all means! The interdependence of nations is an obvious fact today, what? One people can't profit without another's loss, you know."

He is lusty in applause for the "new reign of law and justice throughout the world" that United Nations statesmen so often

"What, again?"

Low © All Countries

talk about; and in the same breath he is lusty in his protests against curtailments of national sovereignty without which it could never be anything but eyewash.

Like everybody else on this island Blimp wishes for lasting peace among nations and a prosperous future for Britain. It is the economic adjustments necessary to the creation of bases for this peace and prosperity that catch him with his towel off. He is suspicious of economists as being in general "Left." "These clever fellers," he sniffs contemptuously. "We don't want clever fellers. We want fellers with brains."

This unfriendly feeling dates from the invention of the Income Tax which he has always regarded as fundamentally unsound, undemocratic and unjust. "You can't limit profits when business is doing well unless you undertake to make up losses when it is doing badly. Well, then, you can't tax a man's income unless you undertake to keep his income up."

Distribution of wealth is a sore point with Blimp. "Since the bulk of the nation's money is held by the masses why should millionaires be taxed more than the masses? Dammit, Sir, answer me that!"

Fooling about with money always moved Blimp to indignation. When economists talk about "developing our resources" he is on his guard at once, fearful of financial blasphemy. Mother Money, like Mother Nature, has her laws which must be left to take their course. Money is the source of all. Labor and soil are all very well, but money is wealth. How Adam ever got on in the Garden of Eden without a bankroll is a mystery.

In the proposals of these economists for constructing prosperity and avoiding slumps after the war he is quick to smell only subversive dodges for that pampering of the lower classes which he used to deplore so in the past. "Full and stable unemployment forsooth! Without unemployment how are we going to get people to work? It doesn't make sense. Security and the abolition of want would sap Initiative and Enterprise. I believe, though I have never experienced it personally, that hunger is a great incentive. Why don't people have Initiative and Enterprise like old Lord So-and-So when he cornered the supply of boots in the last war?"

Social Security and other policies for expanding home markets by raising the standard of living seem to him unsound also. "Industry has to keep the workers—feed, clothe and house them, give them employment to occupy their time," says he. "It can't afford to give them spending money too."

It is on the subjects of Planning and Controls that Blimp becomes most incoherent. He has a fixed idea that all plans, per se, are vague and idealistic. "Gad, Sir, much better to stick to solid realities like Restoring Confidence. Post-war conditions are going to be chaotic. Why confuse them further by Planning?"

He clings as a high moral principle to Private Enterprise, meaning not merely Private Enterprise operating to the desired end of the common good as the planners say they want it to do but Private Enterprise to mess up the nation's affairs too if that seems profitable.

Not that he is unreasonably blind to the usefulness of planning in certain cases. "Some people need to be controlled. Compulsory mobility of labor, for instance, and that sort of thing." After all, in the long run, it depends on who exercises the Control. "Public Control by these dashed politicians and their dashed bureaucrats? Never! Make an awful mess of it. Control by Practical Business Men, now, that is different." Control, that is, without interference or responsibility. In other words, Private Control.

Blimp has sublime confidence in the ability of big bankers and big industrialists to adjust everything to anything, if they are not "interfered with." (Why he should have this confidence Heaven only knows, for their wisdom and foresight have not been remarkable in the past. They did not, for example, see the Slump of 1930 until it hit them on the nose, and their shirts were on Hitler and Hirohito right up to the war. . . . But let that pass.) "Leave 'em alone," says Blimp, "to their merging, their concentrating, consolidating, centralizing of management, expanding of influence abroad, and so on, and all will be well, confidence will be restored and liberty of the Common Man preserved." (The spectacle of Blimp and his Practical Business Men, hardbitten after long years of pestering the Governments for tariffs and subsidies, shouting for "No Interference!" is equaled only by the spectacle of Blimp and his monopolists and chain-store magnates preserving the liberty of the Common Man.)

Unfortunately this dream world, in which Parliament presumably would act as office boy coordinating national policy to the tortuous secret dealings of all the oligarchy of industrial and financial emperors, displays a fatal weakness. Even Blimp sees that it couldn't do the job so long as Labor retains the right to strike. And Labor shows no sign of yielding its privilege to oblige Blimp. The answer to that "situation" takes him on—reluctantly—to a further link in his particular chain of fantasy; coalition of interests, Labor taking a share of management and responsibility. Efficiency, smooth working, and to blazes with the middle classes. Good morning, Fascist!

Blimp doesn't like that prospect at all, but when he is filled with fury at politicians, economists, planners and bureaucrats it seems sometimes the preferable alternative to organization, management and control open and aboveboard for the benefit of the whole people with the executive thereof responsible to the people's representatives duly elected to Parliament. "Gad, Sir, that's not democracy, it's socialism!"

We're all supposed to be fighting a war for Democracy against its opposite, Fascism, but if you want to have a good laugh just ask Blimp to describe and compare the working principles of Democracy and Fascism. "Government of the people, for the people, by the people" signifies three different sorts of people to Blimp: the people who have things done to them, people for whom things are done, and the people whom the latter get to do them.

We still have some Blimps. So have you. But we both have some wise men, too, to keep them in their place. Thank God for that.

Churchill as War Leader: A Reappraisal

by Drew Middleton

LONDON

"WHY, MAN, he doth bestride the narrow world like a Colossus."
So, a dozen years ago, men were inclined to regard Winston
Spencer Churchill, the father of Allied victory in World War II.

Within the last two years, however, Sir Winston's critics,
some of them soldiers of the greatest distinction, have been
attempting to whittle down his massive reputation as a war leader.
This has not altered to any perceptible degree the affection and
respect in which he is held by his countrymen, or, indeed, by the
whole free world. But it does call for a re-examination of Sir
Winston in his dual role of war Prime Minister of the United
Kingdom and one of the chief architects of Allied military and
political policies.

Was he the far-sighted, enterprising, unshakable military leader
and political policy maker the world has accepted? Or, was he
a captious, adventurous, impetuous politician heedless of the
iron realities of war who was kept in check and directed by
sage counsel from professional military leaders? Only history
can give the final answer. The records are incomplete. We know

From the *New York Times Magazine,* February 16, 1958, copyright ©
1958 by The New York Times Company.

nothing yet of what really happened in the Russian high command or in the individual army and army group commands. The German generals' evidence is voluminous but tainted by the fact that most of it has been written at the behest of their conquerors.

Even Sir Winston's monumental work, "The Second World War," leaves one with the sense that something is lacking. The author has given an attentive reader nearly all that is necessary for understanding the conflict as it was fought from these islands on the western edge of Europe: the dispositions of troops, the battle plans, the political forecasts and adjustments, the interplay of political and military personalities, even the directives and memoranda.

Yet to this reader what is missing is the essential genius of Winston Churchill. It is this genius that is being denigrated now and, curiously enough, the book which he intended as the monument to his war effort is the starting place for denigration.

In writing "The Second World War" Sir Winston made free with classified information. This allowed later authors to come on the scene and do the same with their own notes on conferences or plans for battle. Churchill felt it necessary to repeat his wartime judgments; many of these proved unpalatable to distinguished readers. He was and is confident that his policies in both the military and political fields were correct; many differed.

The result has been a spate of autobiographical books by generals on both sides of the Atlantic. As book publishers say, "The generals have returned from the wars to sell their lives—dearly." "Beachcomber," the witty columnist of London's Daily Express, satirized the books criticizing Sir Winston recently. His "Book Review" said:

"General Sir Caxton Bellwether's war memoirs are a warm tribute to his distinguished career. With commendable generosity, while acknowledging the decisive part played by himself and his Service colleagues in every crisis of the war, he admits ungrudgingly that Sir Winston Churchill, though a civilian, made occasional suggestions which were not without value. He goes further and even hints that Sir Winston's influence on events, under the careful guidance of the soldiers, must not be overlooked. It is made clear that, though Sir Winston's energy and pugnacity often disturbed the calmer rhythms of military thought, this must not be taken as an indication that he made no contribution to the final victory."

Sir Winston's most important and severest critic is Field Marshal Viscount Alanbrooke, who, as Chief of the Imperial General Staff, was the Prime Minister's principal military adviser during most of the war. His book is "The Turn of the Tide," based on the Field Marshal's war diaries. It was largely written by Arthur Bryant, a popular historian whose military hero worship, so evident in his comment on Alanbrooke, or Sir Alan Brooke as he was during war, does not extend to Sir Winston.

A second book, less important but equally critical, is "The Business of War," written by Maj. Gen. Sir John Kennedy who served first Sir John Dill and later Alanbrooke in the Operations Section of the General Staff.

Each of these volumes seeks to balance its criticism of Sir Winston by warm salutes to other sides of Sir Winston's leadership. This does not diminish the severity of their criticism of a great man. In fact, the effect is to give the impression that the wartime Prime Minister was important principally as a national cheer leader, capable of inspiring the nation, keeping the House of Commons in order and dealing with Britain's allies while these military literati kept *him* in order and went on with the business of winning the war.

Field Marshal Alanbrooke's criticisms of the wartime Prime Minister are the chief source for the anti-Churchill school of military historians. Since Alanbrooke participated in all the conferences of the Chiefs of Staff, saw much more of Sir Winston man to man and was one of the few Allied field generals to win distinction in the Dunkirk campaign, his words command attention.

From the beginning of their association, Alanbrooke was concerned over the Prime Minister's "appetite for adventurous courses." Although he conceded that his "invincible optimism and power to recoil in disaster" contributed to Sir Winston's national leadership, the general found it interfered with calm planning.

Churchill, he wrote at one point, "was carried away with optimism . . . and established lodgements all round the coast from Calais to Bordeaux with little regard to strength and landing facilities."

This optimism promoted Churchill's love of expeditions, an enthusiasm not shared by Alanbrooke and the other generals. At one favorable juncture in the second Libyan campaign, Alanbrooke found his chief's "far-ranging mind" had envisaged a dazzling series of triumphs—the expulsion of the Germans and the Italians from Tripoli, an invitation from the French authorities to enter Tunisia and Northwest Africa and a descent on Sicily and Sardinia from Malta.

Sir Winston also pleaded "with equal conviction" for a second front in Norway and landings in Italy. At one point, Alanbrooke recalled, the dispatch of land and air forces to operate on the southern flank of the Russian front was "seriously considered." Similar consideration was given, by the Prime Minister at least, to amphibious operations against the tip of Sumatra.

The Prime Minister's impetuosity clearly galled Alanbrooke, who decried his master's "impulsive nature and tendency to arrive at decisions through a process of intuition as opposed to a 'logical' approach." Repeatedly, the Chief of the Imperial General Staff found the Prime Minister "fretting because there is to be no offensive action," not, one would have thought, a particularly grave error in wartime.

Sir Winston's tongue had its rough as well as its eloquent side, and generals got plenty of the former. When he was pressing for an attack on Norway, he was presented with an appreciation of the operation's difficulties by staff officers. To Alanbrooke, Churchill commented, "You have . . . submitted a masterly treatise on all the difficulties and on all the reasons why this operation should not be carried out."

During another conference a general's refusal to accept one of his schemes "started all his worst arguments about generals only thinking about themselves and their reputations and never attacking until matters were a certainty, of never being prepared to take risks."

Both Alanbrooke and Kennedy appear offended by Sir Winston's liking for late hours and odd meal times. They would have been far happier, the reader feels, with a less dynamic leader who treated them with the respect to which they felt the top brass was entitled.

Kennedy's book echoes most of Alanbrooke's criticisms and is vehement about Sir Winston's "interference" and his "interventions in the minutiae of Service affairs." Churchill, Kennedy wrote, "continued to play Tom Tiddler's ground across the dividing line which should properly separate the sphere of the statesman and that of the technical advisers," and added that he has a "deplorable strategic sense." This was at about the time the Prime Minister was goading his generals into action to forestall the German invasion of Iraq.

Kennedy's tight, precise, soldierly mind was shocked by the manner in which Sir Winston took over responsibility for various jobs that, in the general's opinion, should have been left to the commanders in the field. This he carried to the point of listing the number of battalions to be left in overseas garrisons.

Like Alanbrooke, Kennedy was shaken by Churchillian optimism. When Field Marshal Sir Claude Auchinleck's offensive opened in the Western desert, he found the Prime Minister had "magnified the possible result out of all proportion" and "refused to recognize the hard realities of supply in the desert."

Optimism, impetuosity, a love of expeditions—which a layman might translate as a desire to exploit Allied command of the sea to the utmost—and an urge for offensive action: these were Sir Winston's faults. And even when they are described with acidity in Alanbrooke's book or decked out with the gossip of clubland, they do not appear to be real sins.

Any discussion of Sir Winston's real role in the war must be preceded by some appreciation of his past experiences with British generals. As a young officer in the Boer War, as a Cabinet Minister and, briefly, as an infantry officer in the first World War, he came into contact with a collection of generals that included some of the greatest boobies ever to wear uniform. Gallipoli, for which Churchill took the blame, the Somme, Passchendaele were a series of military fiascos then unequaled in British history. In each case some excuse has been made by professional soldiers. The ghastly blood bath of Passchendaele was launched, we are told, because Haig knew the French army had mutinied and the British Expeditionary Force had to keep the Germans engaged. This does not excuse the poverty of imagination, the reactionary tactical sense and the ignorance that went into the actual direction of the battle.

The memories of these disasters bit deep into a generation of British soldiers, as well as into the mind of Churchill.

The generals who were in charge of British and Allied affairs when Churchill became Prime Minister in May, 1940, could not have won his respect. The huge, blustering figure of Field Marshal Ironside was Chief of the Imperial General Staff. In France General Gamelin lived in the midst of a military mystique.

When Gamelin retired into the shadows, after the first German victories, he was replaced by General Maxime Weygand, another of Foch's heirs. General Weygand's attitude from the outset was defeatist.

Under the circumstances then, it is not surprising that Churchill, once he took charge, could restrain his enthusiasm for the military leaders.

Was Churchill wrong to call for action at a time when Britain's resources were low, when her troops were largely untrained and unarmed, when she was alone? I do not believe the historians will find him so. For wars are not won by the careful calculation of forces, by waiting until everyone has enough equipment, until forces are trained to the inch. The British Empire, as Kipling once wrote, would have ended at the Straits of Dover had the army always waited for reinforcements.

It is true that between 1940 and the launching of the invasion of Normandy four years later, the General Staff, led by Dill, Alanbrooke and Kennedy, deflected Churchill from many of his pet projects. There was no invasion of Norway, an operation whose success, in view of the limitations of air power at that time, was highly problematical. Britain's strength was carefully husbanded for the Mediterranean and the European invasions. The generals did intervene between the Prime Minister and sluggish generals in the field, and so the latter had the time—often too much—to regroup and to re-equip.

But none of this affects the position of Churchill as a war

leader. Was he anxious to get to grips with the enemy? There were good reasons for him to be so. Britain's allies looked for active leadership, especially in those dark days when the United Kingdom was the single bastion of freedom.

Was it a military mistake to go into Greece? Perhaps. But was it not political wisdom for Britain, hard pressed though she was elsewhere in the eastern Mediterranean and at home, to come to the help of an ally when she called? Britain's generals, by their own account, were somewhat less than enterprising strategically. They were so engulfed in the monumental problems of raising, equipping and training a new army that they sometimes failed to see that people cannot be asked forever to sacrifice for battles far in the future.

Was the Prime Minister always wrong? No. He was right about Madagascar. The landing there secured bases at a small cost. It looks now as though he was right in his insistence that the Allies should try to get into the Balkans before the Russians.

Did he try to do too much with too little in the Middle East? There is a case for it. But there is also an unanswerable case for Churchill's promotion of British intervention in Iraq which, in the opinion of civil servants on the spot, saved that key nation from German invasion. He understood, far more clearly than many of his critics, the paramount importance of holding the Middle East not only for Britain but for the winning of the war.

Was Churchill occasionally intemperate in his language, short of respect for professional officers of high qualification? I cannot see why this should not be so. There he was, carrying a tremendous burden, greater than that carried by any Englishman in war since Wellington, far greater than any carried by his offended advisers. He had been brought up as a soldier. He was now a politician. Why should anyone think that the Prime Minister, the prop and pillar of Western liberty, should be unduly solicitous of soldiers?

Each criticism may contain a modicum of truth. But, in the end, what does it count against the essential service of the Prime Minister to the cause of freedom? The soldiers served, some of them very notably, one aspect of the battle. He served all.

First opinions are often the best. Over the years mine has persisted: Sir Winston's restless, inquiring mind, his unquenchable optimism, his fierce, almost savage aggressiveness, kept Britain in the war and the war going.

If you were fortunate, you could see him, in 1940, stumping through the shattered streets of London, tears in his eyes and words of consolation and defiance on his lips. It is given to few leaders to reach such identity with the people they serve that the people know, without being told, that the leader and they are one.

Then, a few hours later he would be speaking in the House of Commons, his blurred, raspy voice alternating gibes at the Italian Navy with phrases that surely will live as long as men speak and read English.

And, in between the public appearances, the ceaseless cajoling, driving, planning and brooding encompassing all the problems of all the world.

The memories come crowding back. The dapper figure standing in a garden in Algiers and grinning when someone asked what would happen when the new German submarines entered the Battle of the Atlantic. "I call them U-boats," he said, "and we shall sink them." The surprised, resolute look on his face when Franklin Roosevelt, in another garden at Casablanca, announced the doctrine of unconditional surrender.

I remember best a spring night in Boulogne. The air was heavy with the irrhythmic beat of German bomber motors and beyond them one could discern the crash of the Third Republic. The square below the office was filled with terrified refugees. Out of the darkness of the little room came that stout old voice, offering nothing but blood, toil, tears and sweat. It was as though a hand had been placed at the helm of a great ship driving through wild seas among uncharted rocks.

In assessing the worth of Winston Churchill, it is well to follow the advice of the great Duke of Wellington and look at "the other side of the hill."

"We told the Fuehrer then," a German officer remarked, of 1940, "that all was not satisfactory, that the English would fight and they had Churchill to lead them."

What did Stalin say to Lord Beaverbrook when the latter visited Moscow at one of the war's darkest moments? The cynical, ruthless dictator grunted his appreciation of Churchill, "the old war horse."

Winston Churchill had the greatest capacity for war because he saw it whole. He did not see it as an affair of divisions or destroyer flotillas, fighter squadrons or economic pressures, diplomatic negotiation or political campaigns. He saw it as one, wholly and simply in its basic components.

Keeping in his busy mind the enormous complexity of a world situation, understanding both the thirst of embattled lands for action and the wariness of professionals to engage until everything was ready, feeling the sense of history that pervaded the times, he naturally made mistakes. But compared with the result, they will be seen to be insignificant.

"Who stands if freedom falls?" Who would have stood had Churchill fallen in those years? Was there a better leader for generals and were the generals as omniscient as they now claim to be? Who held the British people together in their hour of trial? Who negotiated and established the grand alliance that finally brought Germany, Japan and Italy, to their knees? We know the answer: Churchill.

When freedom's swords were few he gave them courage and direction. When hearts faltered he restored them. When plans were needed he provided the inspiration. In time he will die. I know he does not worry greatly about the generals and their writings. He is a tolerant man. But it would be a disservice to those who only read about the war if they were to gain the impression that Winston Churchill was anything less than indispensable, that Western civilization would have survived had it not been for him.

"Why, man, he doth bestride . . . ."

England Begins to Step More Briskly

by Anne O'Hare McCormick

LONDON

TO LOOK AT England at this turn from one critical year to another perhaps more critical is to see again that the traditional character and ingrained habits of a people are stronger than its form of government, its material circumstances or the implacable forces of change. You see this better in England than elsewhere because the people are more of a piece. They are molded into a piece by climate, coal, sea frontiers that hold them in and lure them outward, dark cities and gentle landscapes, long discipline in self-government, respect for laws and the rules of cricket and not least by the power and poetry of a great language.

Every time an Act of Parliament is passed representatives of the House of Commons march to the House of Lords, where a royal commission robed in scarlet and ermine and wearing black tricorne hats over their white wigs give assent in the name of the King. The ancient ceremony must date from Norman

From the *New York Times Magazine,* January 4, 1948, copyright ©
1948 by The New York Times Company.

times, for in parts the English text is translated into old French and the royal assent rings out in the original words, "Le roi le veult."

Here is a ritual that means nothing and everything, for it links every successive Member of Parliament and every new bill into the endless chain of parliamentary government. And it is mostly the language that does it. Listening to the words that come echoing down the centuries one cannot help feeling how potent is the majestic mother tongue of the Mother of Parliaments in shaping political attitudes, not merely of England but of the English-speaking world.

Great changes have taken place in England and the cycle of change goes on. In the past year the country touched an all-time low in hardship and depression of spirit. Now rations are down but morale is distinctly up. Most of the rubble of war is swept away and with it the crop of hopes that flourished in the dawn of peace. On this cleared ground you can see better than last year or the year before how much of the pre-war England is gone forever.

Yet what first strikes the returning visitor is not the changes but the things that remain. The most radical revolutions do not plow very deep into the rooted mores of a people, as we see in Russia. The upheaval of the last decade has impoverished Britain, reduced its prestige, lowered its standard of living, put Socialists in power, but it has altered not a bit the qualities—the customs, traits and temper—that made it what it is.

Today England eats less, grumbles more and is more cheerful than it has been since the end of the war. The Conservatives predict that the country will be on near-starvation rations by spring and Laborites point to the rising curve of production, particularly in mines and steel, as a sign that it is climbing back to its old place in the industrial world.

Sir Stafford Cripps, the stern architect of recovery, regards this increase as proof that his austerity program is psychologically as well as economically sound. He remarked to the writer the other day that no one understood this people who did not see the Spartan in the heart of the most comfort-loving Englishman. The British are always at their best, he said, when they are up against it and know they're up against it.

Certainly England steps more briskly than it did. The crowds in the streets look careworn but not listless: they hurry along with an air of purpose, as if at last they are going somewhere. But too many spend too much time standing still. The queue, longer and denser than ever, is not only a feature of the urban scene. It has become so fixed a national habit that people line up when they are not obliged to. For a month, in all kinds of weather, they have stood for hours in mile-long ranks for a glimpse of the royal wedding presents. Thousands wait in queues to see an exhibit of Van Gogh paintings.

Anyone can start a queue by stopping in front of a street vender with a card of elastic or a handful of combs. This is indication enough to a population forever on the hunt that "there's something to be had." Waste of time and energy owing to scarcity is one of the most obvious hindrances to full production.

A murmur of discontent rises from the queues, but so far it is only a murmur. Nobody breaks ranks or jostles his neighbor. English crowds are still the most polite and orderly in the world. Even taxis toe the line by refusing to nose ahead of the car in front. A ring of persons around a fruit stall in the Strand stood patiently this morning while a harassed mother debated the price before buying two small apples for a shilling for her importunate children. Remember hungry-eyed apple sellers begging the careless public to buy during our great depression? Here the shoe is on the other foot.

It is a hungry public that presses for a chance to buy.

The London scene is far brighter than it was. Even in this uncertain peace each month sees more damaged walls patched up, more paint, more roads resurfaced, new taxis, and in the houses more coal fires, more flowers, more lighted windows and polished brass—all the small outward signs of the eternal human impulse to repair the broken fabric of life and start over again.

Theaters and concert halls are full to overflowing and during intermissions tea or coffee still is served to the audience by white-capped maids. Shops are jammed with customers counting their ration coupons more carefully than their cash and scrambling for unrationed goods despite the 100 per cent purchase tax. The basic conditions of recovery are not yet established, economists say, but signs of it are as visible as the faint fuzz of green on the trees when spring is near.

These are superficial impressions of a traveler returning to these misty shores for the third time since the war ended. But what strikes one more as the days go by is the steadiness of England. From a distance you expect to find people cracking under the strain of more privations on top of years of doing without. But the ground is surprisingly firm when you step on it. The national pulse seems to beat more strongly and evenly than before. There is more protest, more questioning of Government measures and methods, the beginning of a black market. To some these are symptoms of new and shocking disrespect for law and authority and to others signs of reviving independence and spirit.

Whatever they mean, however, they do not divide the nation to its depths. With all its differences and stratifications England is essentially a community and this was never so evident as in the peculiar resistance shown by this country to the forces swirling all around it. Except for enemy occupation, everything that has shaken the nations and Governments across the Channel has happened here.

Britain has suffered bombing, devastation, impoverishment, decline of power, a peace as harsh as war. It has passed through what some outsiders describe as a revolution and although this is perhaps too strong a term to apply to the British version of the "New Deal," events have forced an upheaval in the social structure that displaces not only a political party but a long-entrenched ruling class.

Yet the English people are not shaken by the Continental tempest. At the lowest ebb of their fortunes they remain immune to communism and unless the whole world sinks into slavery it is a safe bet that they will always be immune. The stabilizer that holds them steady now and will keep them from going to violent extremes is their long training in the self-discipline of self-government.

But it is not altogether because of temperament or inner equilibrium that battle-scarred London appears less nervous than New York. If there is less sense of danger of war in England than in the United States and less interest in the Continental crises it is because the mass of the population is actually more insulated.

In the Foreign Office they argue that this was always the case and that the people in general are more conscious than ever before of their involvement in world affairs. Certainly there was always a feeling of physical insulation, especially in this gray season when the island is closed in on top from the sun and sky as well as on all sides by the sea and the straits. But in the past this did not prevent the islanders from training their sights on the farthest places and extending their dominion to the ends of the earth.

The atmosphere today is of mental insulation. It is due in large part to straitened circumstances. The thoughts and energies of any nation struggling for economic survival are naturally turned inward. What is not so clear until you see it at first hand is that an economy program as drastic as Britain's imposes restrictions on the mind as well as the body. The Englishman today not only has less to eat and wear than he ever had: he travels less, entertains less, reads less widely, is more out of touch with the outside world.

He is restricted in his movements by the ban on use of gasoline at home and spending money abroad. He has less to smoke and drink and little to share in the way of food, so lives more to himself; for though misery loves company, company doesn't love misery. He sees few foreign films, reads few foreign books and has access to little foreign news. The shortage of newsprint cuts down the supply of all information. University dons and research workers in industry complain they cannot keep up with scientific developments, specialists in fields labeled "nonessential" that they are unable to get material for experimental work. A country that was once the world's great market place is a prime example of the provincializing which is the result of cutting down trade between nations to the bare necessities of existence.

There is more to it than that. A nation's conscious involvement in international affairs is in proportion to its power and the British feel acutely just now that their role is secondary and their voice is not decisive in the great argument over the future of the world. Said a young Labor M. P.: "There is no use getting excited over what happens overseas"—he was referring to the near-by Continent!—"when we can't do anything about it. We have to stand up before we can talk up."

This expresses a widespread sentiment. Last winter the ordinary Briton realized for the first time that the country was really on the rocks. Before that he had about the same dazed attitude toward the economic crisis as he had about the "phony war" early in 1940. Now he is coming back to the mood that prevailed after Dunkerque. He sees "there's a war on," that it is real and that he may lose it. Under that douche of reality he is getting his second wind. Even the Opposition agrees that the ice-water treatment administered by Sir Stafford Cripps in his sober recital of hard facts accompanied by further ration cuts has toned up the flagging spirit of the nation.

Behind the narrow concentration on domestic problems is the instinctive realization that without solvency and self-support Britain can never hope to regain her old international influence. Let no American imagine that the British do not resent dependence on American aid. In every circle, even among those who appreciate and pay tribute to the generous spirit of the United States, it is evident that this is one of the bitterest pills they have to swallow.

They shrug their shoulders over playing second fiddle in the big-power conferences. Today's ruling class has not the Tory tradition of pride in the Empire: it speaks for a people who do not mind getting out of India and are impatient to abandon Palestine, Greece and other strategic bases. But they do want to come back to power in the world.

At the back of their minds and at the back of Labor policy is an ambition to become the balance wheel between East and West. By geographical location and political experience they believe they are best fitted to be in the international sphere the "third force" that divided nations are trying to develop internally. Fully committed though she is at present to Western policy, the long-range aim of Britain is to resume the role of middleman and honest broker, particularly as between the United States and the Soviet Union.

With this aim, it should be noted, goes a good deal of wishful thinking about Russia. It appeared in reaction to the news of the final success of the negotiations for an Anglo-Soviet trade treaty. Although it has since appeared that all concessions to achieve this were made by the British it is hailed by Sir Stafford Cripps and a great part of the public as a sign that the Kremlin may eventually cooperate.

It is just beginning to be understood that the European Recovery Program offers a golden opportunity to re-establish British leadership. Mr. Bevin was the first to respond to Secretary Marshall's initiative. He issued the call to the conference which resulted in Russia's open refusal to participate in organizing a united Europe and the setting up of the sixteen-nation cooperating committee. Britain thus stands at the head of the Western bloc. If she now reconvenes the sixteen and does what she wants to do and can do to direct and inspire the European end of the mutual-aid partnership she is in a position to create that third power needed to restore world equilibrium.

Any report on England at this juncture must stress two points above all. One is that the Marshall plan is now in the first line of British policy. Other plans are filed in the archives while this great idea—the idea of saving Europe from collapse and subjugation—suddenly takes on reality and power. This is the immediate result of President Truman's message to Congress announcing that the plan is not a dream but a practical project and of Secretary Marshall's post-London conference broadcast emphasizing that negotiations for peace have run into a dead end that can be broken through only by action.

The second point is that Britain is on the move again. Revival of the British spirit in the depths of adversity is a bright spot in a clouded world. The British came nearer to defeat this year than they ever did in the war; but now they have taken arms against outrageous fortune and are on a dogged march toward victory. The "talk success" campaign sponsored by The London News-Chronicle meets with an enormous response because people are in revolt against gloom. They want to hear about people working overtime, about prodigies performed by small businesses, about new enterprises and volunteer workers. The British Broadcasting Corporation is starting a series of "progress reports," which will take recording vans to mines, shipyards and farms to collect first-hand stories of how the workers are reaching their targets.

This spurt of will and energy strengthens the Labor Government. At the midterm Labor is not so high in popular favor as it was at the start nor so low as it would have to be to be turned out. The bets are that it will at least live out its five-year term. Even in their hardest hour the English people are a good checkrein on any government. They are set on a course they will not willingly reverse, but while they will not go back to the past neither will they let it go. They are far more resistant to changes in their habits than the more fluid society of the United States and more conservative in their fidelity to tradition.

They are of a piece, in sum, and the piece is woven of strong threads that run unbroken through the centuries.

Despite Austerity, Britain Still Faces a Crisis

by Barbara Ward

LONDON

"WHY DO THE British get all these deficits?" asked Mr. Taber of a newspaper correspondent. "They never used to."

Mr. Taber is not the only puzzled man. At last the debates on Sir Stafford Cripps' budget have come to an end—with all-night sittings in the House of Commons—and the people of Britain are beginning to see the outlines of an economic crisis which they find it almost impossible to accept or even understand.

On the one hand, the performance inside the country has probably never been better. On the other the worst symbol of the economic crisis—the draining away of Britain's last reserves and the scale of the deficit which worries Mr. Taber has grown even worse.

Until 1948 it was still possible to blame part of Britain's economic crisis upon continued inflation which sprang from the Government's determination to do too much with an inadequate national income. But since Sir Stafford decided in April to maintain prohibitive taxation and to budget for a large genuine surplus the signs have been multiplying on every side of the onslaught of a quite severe deflation. The economic face of Britain is changing in the precise way for which every reputable economist has been pleading since 1946. But the external crisis remains.

On the side of Britain's achievements in production and export it is not necessary simply to consult British sources which might well be biased. In recent months an impartial record has been compiled by a competent and independent body, the United Nations Economic Commission for Europe, whose report on economic conditions in Europe is the most comprehensive and factual study yet completed by any organization.

This clear objective document, prepared by British and American and French and Benelux and Polish and Scandinavian experts, represents not the view each Government has of itself but the view which a dispassionate international body takes, having studied all the available facts and figures. And there is no doubt about it. Britain's economic achievement in the last three years has been striking and its economic stability almost unequaled; in terms of output, it leads Europe.

Taking 1938 as the normal year, industrial output in Britain at the end of 1946 was 15 per cent above the 1938 level, and after a decline during the fuel crisis of February, 1947, climbed back to roughly the same level by the end of the year. In the same period Belgian production never reached more than a 6 per cent increase, France 4 per cent, Sweden 4 per cent, Denmark 8 per cent. The only equal achievement is that of Denmark, which in the second quarter of '47 secured a 19 per cent increase (which, however, fell to 6 per cent in the next quarter). Since this index is the clearest general guide to economic activity, it can be said that British production is the highest in Europe.

The record in the sphere of foreign trade is even more remarkable. Alone among the European nations (with the possible exception of Finland) Britain has vastly increased its exports and has as drastically cut its imports in comparison with the pre-war trading pattern. Every other nation has allowed its exports to fall sharply and many of them have swollen imports. For instance, in 1947 Sweden, Norway, France and Belgium imported 20 to 30 per cent more than in 1938 and exported between 20 to 30 per cent less. But the figure for Britain is a drop in imports of over 20 per cent and an increase in exports of nearly 16 per cent (which today is nearer 40).

Another index—this time not for production but of stability—is to be found in Britain's budgetary position. As the report points out, Britain was in 1947 the only European nation with the exception of Sweden to avoid a budget deficit. In Belgium it had risen to 40 per cent above pre-war, in Holland to 148 per cent, in Norway to 29, in France to 26. This year Sir Stafford Cripps has budgeted for a big surplus—$1,320,000,000—as the surest method of combating inflation. The report also illustrates statistically the value of this policy in terms of stable retail prices, a controlled circulation of currency and the maintenance of the buying power of sterling. Once again, the record stands almost unchallenged in Europe.

What, then, has gone wrong? In terms of 1938, Great Britain should be enjoying a prosperity such as it had never known before, with its people fully employed for the first time since 1918, with production high above the pre-war level, with exports soaring, with sound finance. But quite obviously the country is not passing through a phenomenal burst of prosperity. Food and clothing are more drastically rationed than during the war. High taxation is virtually unchanged. The pressure on housing has not diminished much and in all classes of society there is a certain exasperation at the long continuing rigors of "siege economics."

The situation, it is true, is not so uncomfortable or hopeless as some prosperous visitors abroad would have people believe. Indeed, for the lowest third of the population the position is a vast improvement on the underfed, unemployed decade which preceded the war. But the constant economic pressure of rationing and taxation continues and with it the feeling of bewilderment and unease.

What *is* the matter? What has gone wrong? Why do we have record exports—yet a new tax on beer? Why do we produce more iron and steel than ever before—yet pay more for tobacco? Why do we have a budget surplus—and yet a new tax in the shape of something very close to a capital levy? The disparity between performance and reward might puzzle anybody. It certainly puzzles—and exasperates—the British man in the street.

The chief difficulty in explaining an economic situation is the number of different factors which influence it. What young Jack Bull in the pub and Mr. John Bull in the directors' meeting tend to want is the short answer—"It's all because of the capitalists and profiteers." "It's all because of the Labor Government." "It's all the Jews." "It's all the Germans." "It's the Americans." "It's Stafford Cripps." But an economic crisis as intense and prolonged as that of Britain is never "all due" to any one thing. It is a complex business and there are no short answers. But two reasons above all explain why, although Britain's internal achievement stands comparison with any in the world, its economic crisis is if anything more acute than ever. Unhappily both reasons lie beyond Britain's power to set them right, at least in the short term.

The core of its difficulties is the appalling disequilibrium in its balance of payments. The excess of imports over exports in 1947 was in the neighborhood of $1,809 million. The need to fill this gap by smaller imports and higher and higher exports goes far to explain the chief symptom of Britain's internal crisis—the shortage of goods which prolongs the need for rationing and the pressure of purchasing power on goods which creates inflation.

But how did the gap arise? This brings us to the first explanation for Britain's crisis and it is in many ways a disappointingly simple one. It is the war—or rather two wars in a generation in both of which Britain was the only nation to come in on the first day and stay until the last. The war was responsible for direct shortages, for the present need for capital re-equipment, for the disorganization of the labor market which drew workers away from the mines and the textile industries and now makes it so difficult to coax them back.

But above all the war destroyed the largest single prop of

the British economy—its enormous income from overseas investments and from invisible items such as shipping, banking and insurance. The latter earnings will no doubt be restored in time, even if not to the same degree. But the capital investment which was spent without stint to finance the early stages of the war has gone for good and the conditions for rapid capital accumulation are not so good as to allow hopes that new investment will take the place of the old.

To go back once more to the Economic Commission's Report, it gives in dramatically clear terms the different economic facts of Britain in 1919 and 1920 and in 1946 and 1947. In both periods the internal difficulties were much the same, although the recovery of production has been more rapid this time and industrial peace incomparably greater. The external surplus of imports over exports was almost as great—$2,252 million for 1919 and 1920, $2,612 million for 1946 and 1947. But in 1919 and 1920 Britain was cushioned by its vast overseas investments. In 1946 and 1947 not only had its income dwindled almost to nothing but what little remained was swallowed up in expenditure on military responsibilities abroad—in Indonesia, in Palestine, in Germany—to the tune of $2 billion.

Here are the figures. They speak for themselves. For 1919 and 1920 Britain's income from various invisible items, including investments, amounted to $2,560 million and against it, Government expenditure abroad on military occupation and so forth amounted to only $28 million. For 1946 and 1947 Britain's invisible income amounted to only $608 million, and this was canceled out by Government expenditure abroad to the tune of $2,216 million.

What was the result? For 1919 and 1920 Britain's external accounts balanced, leaving a surplus of about $280 million. For 1946 and 1947 the deficit was the appalling figure of $4,220 million—a figure which helps to explain the rapid swallowing up of the American loan, the continuing crisis at home, the shortages, the stringency; above all, it explains the need for further American assistance if the people of Britain are not to end 1948 starving and workless.

A deficit of over $4 billion means national bankruptcy, and if the British people were given to introspection and self-pity it would be a bitter thought that the factor more responsible for their penury than any other was their whole-hearted waging of two wars. But, mercifully, the British have little tendency to brood on their misfortunes, and in any case, wars are not the whole story.

The other factor is the extremely unfavorable character of the current "terms of trade." Terms of trade is a short-hand way of expressing the relationship between the cost of imports and the value of exports. When a given volume of exports buys a proportionately large amount of imports the terms are favorable. When a much larger proportion of exports has to be sold to buy a given amount of imports, terms are unfavorable.

In the Thirties the terms of trade were consistently favorable to Britain since raw materials and foodstuffs were cheap and industrial exports were relatively more costly. But since the end of the war foodstuffs and raw materials have been sought for desperately by every importing nation. Prices have skyrocketed, and although industrial exports have also commanded high prices the much higher cost of imports added an extra $1.2 billion to Britain's import bill in 1947.

Today the situation is even more critical. Between the end of 1947 and the end of April the price index for imports rose by 6 per cent, the index for exports by only 3 per cent. The British are faced with the prospect of paying even more for their imports in 1948, and there are disturbing signs that the boom in the market for industrial goods is beginning to slacken.

These two reasons set together—the loss of pre-war income and the unfavorable terms of trade—more than answer Mr. Taber's question: "Why do the British have these deficits?" They leave unanswered the question what Britain unaided can do about it.

The scale of the economic crisis in Britain has inevitably led people abroad—and in Britain itself—to query whether a real recovery is possible. Many ask whether the loss of wealth and the disruption of old trading patterns have not been too great to allow Britain to restore its position. But the answer surely is not that Britain is incapable of restoring its economic stability but that it cannot restore the *same* type of stability as it enjoyed before the war. Britain cannot restore its old position—that has vanished under the hammer blows of world war—but it can build a new one.

The task is double. At home it means a new concerted effort to revive British economic efficiency, to modernize, to mechanize, to undo the conservative industrial policies of the war years and to end the restrictionist attitude of both management and labor. This is a hard program, but it is not impossible, and the goal of doubling of British productivity in the next five years is part of the answer.

The other part is wider. It consists of taking the lead in a new economic pattern in Western Europe. The breathing space offered to the European nations by American generosity in the shape of the Marshall Plan can be used to make the restoration of productivity and efficiency in Britain part of the wider program to revive the productivity of Western Europe by creating a "Western Union" free from irrational tariff barriers, from nationalist obstacles to the nationalization and reorganization of industry and from all the inhibitions which must exist between sixteen separate national economies and which do not exist—mercifully—in the wide continental economy of the United States.

The details of such a program cannot be discussed here. Its working out creates special problems for Britain, with its imperial commitments. But the point is that the existence of new possibilities in Western Europe and the fact of an industrial slack to be taken up in Britain itself do offer the hard-pressed community ways out of its present crisis and do show light at the end of the long tunnel the British have been tramping through since the war ended.

It is true that the pursuit of both objectives demands vision, courage, hard work and pertinacity, but these virtues have in the past come again and again to the assistance of the British people. Thrust out of Europe six centuries ago, they created the first empire in America. Thrust out of America, they opened up Africa and India. Crippled by colonial and European wars, they chanced upon the "industrial revolution." Now, outstripped by America in the industrial race, they can find new opportunities in a European partnership. The tradition of resource and adaptability exists. And the British, as all the world knows, are a traditional people.

Appraisal of Britain's Welfare State

by Richard H. Fry

LONDON

THE BRITISH PEOPLE have gone farther than any other modern industrial nation in making life secure for all. They have also got into a dangerous international squeeze of being unable to pay for the imports their overcrowded island must have to maintain any Western standard of living. No question excites more controversy in England and the outside world than this: Are the two facts cause and effect? Has the creation of the welfare state prevented the country from paying its way in the world?

Some of our American critics seem to have found a simple answer. They tell us—and quote some of our own writers in support—that the workers will never work hard enough if the state gives them a guaranteed minimum of food, housing, clothing, and medical attention, including even a free funeral. They tell us that the removal of fear removes the incentive to betterment. They tell us that the crushing taxation necessary to provide all these free services is bound to kill business incentive and enterprise.

From the *New York Times Magazine,* September 25, 1949, copyright © 1949 by The New York Times Company.

Devaluation of the pound sterling will not affect the main services of the welfare state. But it may be the prelude to some trimming of welfare expenditure, permitting a cut in present crushing tax rates. To get the full benefit of devaluation Britain will have to produce more and export more. That will not be done unless the Government reduces its own demands for labor and productive facilities for social service purposes; and unless taxation, which paralyzes the will to work, is lessened.

The experiment, which began in 1909 (after two decades of a public debate which still reverberates throughout the globe) with Lloyd George's social security budget, was launched in full knowledge of man's natural weakness. Forty years of advance toward the complete welfare state have strengthened the original doubts but have not shaken the basic faith that Britain is nearer to the ideal society than any other large modern country.

There is no simple answer, in fact, to the question whether the British concern with welfare has caused the country's economic difficulties. After the first World War deflation, unemployment and bankruptcy were fully tried out in Britain as incentives. They had some effect but they left all classes of the population numbed with fear.

By the time the Twenties ended, both management and labor were filled with an overwhelming desire for security, stability, relief from pain. In the ten years preceding the second World War the craving for stability dominated British public life. Governments of the Left and the Right—and remember the Conservatives were in power nearly all the time—increasingly accepted the idea that the state had to provide jobs and comforts when business could not.

Unemployment insurance has existed in England for nearly forty years; unemployment pay beyond the insurance period has been paid for twenty-five years. Free medical treatment has been available to every British citizen with an income of less than $1,600 a year for a generation. Such additional services as free milk for school children and state subsidies for low-rent houses were introduced and extended by Tory governments before the recent war. Up to that time it was generally believed that the generous social services provided by the British state, while they might take the edge off the competitive struggle, more than offset that deficiency by creating contentment, fitness, and social stability.

Let me stress this point. The same American critics who think the latest extravagances of our welfare state border on insanity, often admire the unique social cohesion of the British community. Surely the two things are linked. Leaving aside a few recent stupidities on which everybody agrees and which are certain to be put right, the welfare state has made "two nations" into one. The fact that in moments of national danger there is always a common national response cannot be unconnected from the fact that poor and rich feel themselves to be part of a community which "looks after them."

All this is meant to emphasize that the controversy should be limited to the most recent advance of welfare economics in Britain. That this advance has been too sudden for the human weaknesses of most people is now almost universally admitted. That it has been too costly for the financial position of the country at the moment is no longer denied by anybody. The trouble is that this has become a party political subject. The 1945 election was won on social services, not on socialism. The Government fears to lose votes if it cuts any of the services now. The Tory opposition fears to lose votes unless it promises to do at least as much for the ordinary man as the Labor party has done. It is this political dilemma which is dangerous. It may prevent the next Government, whatever its color, from bringing the whole system back to earth.

I do not believe there is any need to go back on the main propositions of the welfare state which were well established before World War II, or even on the principal advances made during and since the war. I do not believe that the main benefits of the welfare policy, if introduced at reasonable intervals and with due regard to cost, cause people to slacken at their work. The experiment has been carried forward too fast and too far in the last five years—that is the real issue in dispute.

The foundations of the post-war advance were laid during the war and accepted by Mr. Churchill's coalition Government. It is true that Mr. Churchill himself, though an old and still ardent liberal (he hates the typical Tories like poison), probably tolerated these sweeping welfare proposals merely as a means of binding the workers closer to the national cause. But that is precisely the advantage of these policies in time of peace as well as of war.

At any rate, it was under Mr. Churchill's Government that the state was made for the first time responsible for maintaining a "high and stable level of employment" (the fashionable phrase "full employment" has never been mentioned in any official British document). It was at that time that Lord Beveridge was commissioned to devise the plan of a comprehensive national insurance for all citizens, to cover unemployment, old age, sickness and funeral costs. The greater part of the Labor Government's welfare legislation since 1945 is based on the famous series of "Plans," published by the coalition Government during the war.

Today the Englishman is offered—in return for his taxes, local rates, and national insurance contribution—a wide range of benefits: free education; medical attention, including medicines, spectacles and the now-famous false teeth; family allowances for each child except the first; free milk for school children; a fixed weekly payment in times of sickness or unemployment—as a right, not as charity; a pension in old age, and a funeral free of charge. In addition the Government's financial policy keeps basic foodstuffs artificially cheap, subsidizes low rents, and provides work for many who might be out of a job on purely commercial grounds.

Has all this made life too easy? For the moment undoubtedly, yes! The lower-paid worker can stay in bed when he has a headache, or take a week's holiday, without losing much. The difference between his wage (less tax) and his state benefit is not quite enough to overcome the weakness of the flesh. Until a year ago when the new Health Service came into operation, industry was plagued by "voluntary absenteeism"; now the more serious trouble is "involuntary absenteeism"—workers (especially women) staying away from work with a medical certificate.

But one can easily make too much of that. I find all my American friends convinced that the British worker has gone over to the forty-hour week. That is quite untrue. The average time actually being worked by civilian workers in British industry is 45.3 hours a week; if you exclude women, boys and girls, the average for men over 21 years is 46.7 hours a week. In 1938 it was exactly one hour more. That is the extent of the shortening. A great deal of it is explained by the progress in mechanization and the expansion of mass production industries during those eleven years. Far more of it is explained by the difference between the semi-depression of 1938 and the boom of 1949.

The bargaining position of labor in England at this time was bound to be very strong, whatever Government was in power. The economic situation is dominated by the need to reconstruct war damage, to expand production so as to make good the loss of overseas investments, and to catch up with the wartime arrears of capital replacement and modernization. In these five post-war years there was bound to be full employment; there were bound to be more jobs than men. It did not need the welfare state to weaken the workers' incentive.

This means that we have had no real test of the effects of the welfare policy. In the conditions of the last four years labor might have behaved exactly the same way if there had been no social security, no national health service, and none of the other recent innovations. It is just the same with nationalization; no one can honestly say that the change of stock ownership from private to public hands has made the nationalized services and industries less efficient than they would have been in the post-war conditions in any case. There has not been time.

Nor is there any proof that the threat of further nationalization is deterring industry from making all the new capital investments it would have made otherwise. In steel, for instance, there has not been so much enterprise and so much expenditure on new plant and equipment for thirty years.

So long as there was a seller's market for British exports in the world there was bound to be a seller's market for British labor at home. It is quite impossible to judge objectively how much this economic fact has been responsible for the complaints made by British business men, and how far the human failings have been encouraged by the policies of the Government.

But taking the two influences together, one can certainly affirm that the post-war circumstances have not been favorable to an all-out human effort in Britain. Progress toward full economic recovery has, I think, been hampered in varying degrees by five distinct influences.

(1) Excessive strain on manpower and material resources, with consequent inefficiency, has been caused by the various social projects enforced by the Labor Government—such as the accelerated building of schools, hospitals and low-rent houses at a time when the rebuilding and extension of industrial plants should have had priority.

(2) Shortening of the average work week from 46.5 hours in 1938 to 45.3 hours, and that for men alone from 47.7 to 46.7 hours. This is partly due to the expansion of the mass-production industries but even so the situation demanded longer weeks, not shorter ones.

(3) Nationalization, while it may have had little effect so far on efficiency, has certainly distracted public attention into political controversy, and stirred up bitterness, at a time when united concentration on economic recovery was the overriding need.

(4) The sense of security has certainly grown beyond a healthy limit. There was great need for it to grow: extreme insecurity of employment had been the most prolific cause of restrictive practices and general slacking for twenty years before the recent war. But the post-war boom, plus the Government's inflationary policy, plus vastly increased social services, have brought many people, especially the young ones, to think that they need not take much trouble in life. However, the degree to which the mass of experienced workers really believe in this security of the job is easily exaggerated. It is inflation, with full employment, which is most hampering in the badly needed process of shifting labor to the more efficient industries and of lowering costs.

(5) Far more damaging than any of these factors, however, has been excessive taxation. That is really where the British

system is bogging down. From top to bottom, from millionaire to miner, people are sick and tired of the present weight of taxes. The worker refuses to do a few hours overtime because the extra pay attracts the full rate of income tax. The business man drops a project that involves some risk because his company keeps only 40 per cent of the profit, and he himself, if subject to super-tax, may get only a small fraction of the final dividends. The Government takes 40 per cent of the national income in taxes. That is more than any democratic nation can stand without ceasing to care.

Heavy taxation is inevitable in England. Even at artificially cheapened interest rates the service of the national debt takes 6 per cent of the national income; together with the cost of defense and of payments on war-damage claims this comes to well over 15 per cent of the national income. If we cut out all social services and subsidies the total tax burden would still have to be at least 25 per cent of the national income. And you could not cut so deeply without tremendous and lasting dislocation.

But it is one thing to say that taxes must be very heavy and quite another thing to say that they cannot be reduced from the present level. The cost of the social services in the current financial year is around $4.5 billion. This pays for education, national insurance, national health service, housing subsidies and family allowances. The food subsidies, which are also a kind of social service, add another $2 billion.

The bulk of this money is paid by the taxpayer, both direct and indirect. (The insurance contributions of employers and employes provide about $1.25 billion.) Taking only that part which is provided by the state it will amount this year to roughly two-fifths of the total tax revenue. It is obvious that even a moderate reduction in the social services, which is all that has been seriously discussed, would substantially lighten the tax burden and revive incentives.

Just who pays for the social services is a matter of hot dispute. It happens that the yield of income tax and surtax, which fall more heavily on the higher income brackets, is almost exactly the same in the current budget estimates as the yield from customs and excise taxes, which fall more heavily on the mass of the population. The distinction is, of course, only a matter of degree. Several million weekly wage-earners pay income tax; for many millions of professional and business people the indirect taxes add heavily to their household bills. Here is a list of customs and excise receipts as estimated for the fiscal year 1949-50:

Tobacco	£ 625,000,000
Beer	280,000,000
Wines and Spirits	110,000,000
Food	20,000,000
Entertainments	45,000,000
Purchase Tax	250,000,000
Other	170,000,000
Total	£1,500,000,000

Some remarkable facts arise from this little table. The state takes in purchase tax alone as much as it spends on subsidizing the new National Health Service and cheap housing taken together. It takes in taxes on beer and tobacco almost four times as much as it spends on education and twice as much as it spends on the whole of the social security system. Or to put it in another way: if you grant that something like two-thirds of the beer and tobacco taxes are paid by those sections of the people who benefit most from the social services, you can safely say that they pay the entire cost of the subsidies to food prices and to the health service themselves when they hand over their shillings to buy a packet of cigarettes or a glass of beer.

Here is the key to the high cost of living of which the British labor unions complain. If the taxes on tobacco and drink (£1,-015,000,000) were halved and the food subsidies (about £500,-000,000) were abolished, the cost of living would remain exactly the same. The Government raises an excessive amount of taxation which paralyzes the spirit of all classes, and it hands a great part of the revenue directly back to the taxpayers by lowering the prices of certain goods and services, and providing other services "free."

Up to a point, the British would undoubtedly rather have services than money. That decision was made long ago and remains unshaken. It is also accepted that heavier taxes should be paid by the wealthier classes so that social security and other benefits should be provided for those with less money. These policies are agreed between the parties. What is in question is the degree. The point to which this policy can be driven without becoming nonsensical has been left behind. The greater part of the people who are being supported and subsidized now have to pay for these advantages themselves. Money is taken out of your left-hand pocket to be put back into your right-hand pocket.

That is the excess of zeal which is weakening the cause. There is no doubt at all that both sides of the ledger will have to be deflated before long. Sir Stafford Cripps made it pretty clear in his last budget speech in April that he was in favor of pricking the bubble. If he gets back into office after the next elections he may do it. Otherwise another Government will.

To put this into figures: Most British economists now agree that the £3,250,000,000 government expenditure has to be cut back by roughly £500,000,000. This can be done by halving the food subsidies, saving something on the health service and ordinary administrative expenditure, reducing the housing and other capital subsidies and postponing some public capital expenditure, such as school building. This cut would make it possible to: cut income tax by one shilling in the pound; remove the tax on undistributed profits and moderate some other inequities; cut beer and tobacco duties by 20 per cent and halve the purchase tax.

Whether it is done in this particular way is a matter for political bargaining. But that the demoralizing tax burden caused by the attempt to disguise the state as a fairy godmother could be easily relieved in some such way is certain. A minor operation of this kind which would leave no one any worse off would be sufficient for a time to restore the incentive of gain to the

British economic system. It would leave the welfare state slightly shorn of its latest trappings, but still well alive.

Other problems would then take the limelight. Britain has enough of them to face without slowing down her pace by expensive luggage. If the spirit revives and circumstances bring us a little luck for a change, production and exports may gradually reach a level at which the present social services would no longer seem too expensive.

Report on Britain's "Cradle-to-Grave" Plan

by Herbert L. Matthews

LONDON

THE GREATEST experiment in social service ever attempted by a democratic Government—Britain's "cradle-to-grave" National Health Service—has been in operation for six months. That is too short a time to pronounce it a success or a failure, but not too short to describe and assess its early life.

It is yowling with aches and pains, but all things considered, one must account it a lusty infant.

American critics or champions who look across the Atlantic for arguments to oppose or support President Truman's plan to introduce compulsory health insurance will find whatever they are seeking. The American Medical Association will be able to produce a mass of testimony from British doctors on how badly the scheme is working. Conversely, the Federal Security Administration should be able to compile a still more formidable body of testimony from patients, druggists, dentists and many doctors to prove that a nation of nearly fifty million can take care of the health of every man, woman and child from teething to senility.

This old country has frequently shown a genius for new ideas, and it was natural that a Socialist Government should decide that a scheme which was designed to benefit 95 per cent of the people ought to be good. However, no one expected a colossal and revolutionary plan of this sort to function smoothly and efficiently in only six months. Even a generation is a brief period in the life of a nation. At this early date, one merely has the right to report the way the scheme is working now, to list the opposing arguments, and to analyze the effects of the service to date on doctors, patients and the general health of the country.

But, first, one must know what it is all about.

The actually ill could always be taken care of free in Britain, and there has been compulsory national health insurance for virtually all workers since 1911. However, wives and children had to pay doctor's bills, and only half of the insured workers used to qualify for dental services.

Now everybody gets everything, so to speak. Doctors and dentists, specialists and hospitals, maternity and child welfare, home nursing, spectacles, dentures, wigs, deaf aids, artificial legs and other necessary appliances as well as all drugs and medicines are yours for the asking. You can have a baby, break a leg, get a toothache and go insane, and it won't cost you a penny of direct outlay.

Yet despite the scope of this program medical treatment here remains outwardly unchanged. Doctors keep their same offices. Patients come in as before and wait their turn, or the doctor goes to their homes as he did when they were private patients. Hospitals and clinics are carrying on without the slightest difference so far as anyone can see. For his medicines, the patient still takes his prescription to the druggist of his choice.

Everyone under the health scheme is entitled to choose his doctor and change him at will. Doctors can accept or reject anybody. The scheme is completely voluntary, and the public and practitioners alike can stay out of it if they wish.

It is what might be called the mechanism of administration that has changed. Most Britons today belong to the "national insurance" plan and every such insured person pays 4 shillings 11 pence (slightly under $1) per week by buying proper stamps at any postoffice. Of that amount, 8½ pence (less than 15 cents) goes to the National Health Service; the rest is for old-age and widows' pensions, and unemployment, sickness and disablement benefits.

You can join the health scheme whether you are insured or not. If insured, you continue paying your "4 and 11" and nothing more. If you elect to register for the health service and are uninsured, you pay nothing. In either case, you have no other financial medical worries unless you want some extra fancy eyeglass frames or an expensive hearing aid. Employers make a small contribution to the health scheme, but five-sixths of the total cost comes from the national budget. Higher income taxes take up part of the slack.

It is, therefore, the Government that settles all bills on behalf of the patient. Doctors, dentists, druggists and the like get quarterly checks from the Government, instead of being paid as they go along by their clients.

Such is the scheme that Britain's dynamic and sharp-tongued Minister of Health, Aneurin Bevan, pushed through Parliament and got working last July 5. He fought it out with doctors and dentists, meeting just such opposition as the AMA is now mustering in America, and, while it was universally agreed that he was high-handed, tactless and ruthless, it was an unequal struggle, since the Government has a safe majority in Parliament and could push the health bill through.

Now "Nye" Bevan is feeling moderately well pleased with himself and his National Health Service. It is creaking and groaning, but it is under way and gathering steam. In fact, some of the difficulties arise because it is almost too successful.

Out of an estimated total of 21,000 general practitioners in England and Wales, more than 18,000 agreed voluntarily to join the scheme. There are about 10,000 dentists here, and 8,700 of them have joined up. Of the 14,000 chemists, as druggists are called here, virtually all are in the health service.

Most impressive of all are the figures for patients. The population of England and Wales is about 43 million. Well over 40 million have registered with doctors, the remainder being mainly well-to-do and elderly who carry on with their old family physicians on a paying basis.

(These figures are limited to England and Wales because the original bill covered only those two political divisions. Similar bills have been passed separately for Scotland and Northern Ireland, and the situation is virtually the same there.)

As the figures suggest, the British public in general likes the new scheme. Demands of all kinds have been so great that Mr. Bevan had to make a public plea recently for everybody to go easy. The luxury, so to speak, of enjoying bad health without paying for it has been irresistible.

Some abuses have been reported. Patients are suspicious that they aren't getting the same treatment now, although they really are, and ask more of doctors than they did before. A Scottish ear doctor recently told of a man who, having already got two pairs of spectacles and a denture from the state, asked him for a hearing aid to complete his outfit, although he wasn't deaf. An optician wrote to a British medical journal that "I have discovered that in a southwest town a considerable number of brand-new spectacles have been located in pawnshops."

Dishonesty, however, is rare. What has happened in the case of spectacles, for instance, is that many thousands who would have gone without them or bought them—as Britons did to an amazing extent—in 5-and-10-cent stores, now get proper glasses after examination by an oculist.

Typical of the general reaction to the scheme is the attitude of young Mistress Doris Collier whose husband, a clerk, pays his "4 and 11" weekly. She says she likes it much better now.

Not being insured, Mistress Collier used to have to go to a district nurse and to pay for pre-natal care. Now she is getting better care for her coming child and getting it free along with a weekly grant for thirteen weeks and a lump sum of £4 when the baby is born.

Evelyn, who will be 2 "next Sunday week," is Mistress Collier's other chief reason for rejoicing. When Evelyn had enteritis a year ago she nearly died before they took her to the clinic. Last week, Evelyn was taken to the family doctor—at no cost to the family—because she had a cold and was sniveling.

The medical effectiveness of the National Health Service is more difficult to assay than its popularity. There have been no epidemics this winter, and except for one fog that lasted five days, no weather calamities to put undue strain on the profession. Everyone connected with the service itself insists that it is too soon to pass judgment on the country's health after only six months.

Nevertheless, certain specifics cannot help but be noticed. There can be no question that medical attention, medical appliances and medicines are more widely distributed than ever before. Spectacles, already mentioned, are a case in point. Before the new act took effect Britons used four to five million pairs of spectacles annually. The present demand is estimated by representatives of the ophthalmic industry at a little under eight million pairs.

There is a similar story for medicines. Britain's "chemist's shops" are now dispensing nearly 100 per cent more prescriptions than a year ago. In the old days doctors hesitated to prescribe expensive medicines like penicillin and sulfa drugs, knowing that the patients couldn't afford them, but now they not only can do so but are tempted to prescribe large doses in order to postpone the next visit from the patient. Because the doctor's pay is based on the number of patients rather than the number of "calls," it is to his advantage to do preventive work, a practice which also benefits the patient.

Finally, since records must be kept of every visit and every patient, Britain in the next generation is going to have a national medical record unequaled in the history of the science.

From the doctor's viewpoint, the plan has both advantages and disadvantages. Doctors are given the choice of being paid entirely by so-called capitation fees amounting to about 17 shillings 6 pence (about $3.46) annually for each patient on their panels or they can accept a fixed annual payment of £300 (about $1,210) plus a capitation fee of 15 shillings 2 pence (about $3) for each patient. No doctor may handle more than 4,000 panel patients.

There are many possibilities for adding to basic earnings. Doctors can continue to take private patients and charge their usual fees. They get extras for maternity cases and for special work on medical boards and in clinics.

On the average, it is conceded that remuneration is fair, and it was, indeed, fixed by a committee composed half of doctors and half of laymen. However, it is natural that distinguished physicians and specialists and those with especially lucrative practices are losing out, and in general the scheme favors the younger doctors against the older ones with established practices.

Typical of these young doctors whose careers as medical men will be pursued under the National Health Service is J. Leslie MacCallum. Dr. MacCallum's office, or surgery, as the Britons call it, is in the Bloomsbury district of London. He has 2,100 patients and doesn't see how any doctor can give proper service to many more than that.

Dr. MacCallum's panel runs from the very poor to the professional middle classes, who live by the thousands in Bloomsbury. He feels he must treat them all as if they were private patients, and he encourages them to join the health scheme. They can telephone and make appointments to go to his surgery, or, if they are confined to bed, he visits them just as he did before July 5.

For anyone in his early thirties like MacCallum, who was just starting to build up a practice, there was really no choice but to join the health scheme. Anyway MacCallum, while critical, believes that it is a democratic scheme with possibilities of preventive health services on a vast scale for the nation.

"It is surprising how much illness that used to remain undisclosed and unchecked, particularly among women, has come to light in the last six months," he says. On the other hand, he worries because he can't give as much attention and service to each patient as he would like.

Like all doctors, MacCallum was dismayed at the smallness of the first quarterly installments from the Government last September which, because the quarter was a short one and because some items were temporarily withheld, turned out to be less than everyone expected. Most doctors are living on loans from their banks, but the kinks in the payment plan are being smoothed out.

If doctors have been busy since July, dentists are frantic with work. Unlike the doctors, there aren't enough dentists to go around and nobody can register with the dentists. There is a priority for children, maternity cases and emergencies; otherwise you wait your turn.

It is a well-known fact that when a Briton has a toothache, he waits until he can stand it no longer and then goes to a dentist and has the tooth yanked out. When a number of teeth have been pulled he is in the satisfactory state—to him—of being able to get the rest extracted so that he can have a denture made.

The result, now that dentures are free, is to give the impression of an impatient population queuing up to get their teeth pulled and dentures made. The Socialist Government seems to be realizing the prophecy of the Scottish divine who was asked how there could be gnashing of teeth for toothless sinners. "Teeth will be provided," he replied.

Because of the shortage of dentists and the demand for their services, dentists' earnings have rocketed into the big money. The Ministry of Health had it figured out that the average dentist working some 1,500 hours a year would earn £1,600. Instead, dentists are working on the whole about 3,000 hours and, with extra remuneration for special services, are making from £4,000 to £10,000 annually in many cases.

Mr. Bevan's Ministry announced new regulations limiting those earnings only a week ago, a move which annoys the dentists who point out that the income tax extracts from 40 to 65 per cent of their earnings. The danger, of course, is that they will simply take less patients and leave more toothaches. Another danger is that the public dental services for school children may be wrecked if dentists quit for private practice.

The strongest opposition to the National Health Service exists, as might be expected, among the doctors. The British Medical Association debated the issue heatedly for a few years. At first it advised doctors to stay out, but when Mr. Bevan, who had antagonized the doctors by his high-handedness, made some concessions, there was a close vote in favor of advising doctors to join. However, a diehard group has set up a dissident wing to fight on.

Doctors and dentists who stay out of the health service simply carry on as before. Specialists and those with well-to-do clients and long-established practices can manage, although they earn less.

They were surprised and disconcerted when more people joined the health scheme than they had expected, leaving fewer private patients. However, the doctors who stayed out were obviously those who could afford to do so.

One of the most repeated arguments of the opposition group concerns the high cost of the plan. It is a fact that the cost of the scheme far exceeds the official estimates, and is proving a great worry.

The original estimate in the Parliament bill for the first year was £152,000,000 (about $612,000,000). When the time came to make up the civil estimates for the 1948-49 figure, it was raised to £218,000,000. The actual cost will be fully £240,-000,000, which is getting close to a billion dollars—a tidy budgetary sum for Sir Stafford Cripps to find.

A more fundamental controversy is being fought out on the quality of the service that can be rendered. Lord Horder, who was physician to the royal family and is one of Britain's most distinguished doctors, has been leading this battle.

"A variation on a current gibe," he recently wrote, "might be to say that we seem likely to get not only the best Government, but also the worst medicine that money can buy."

No medical man or woman, Lord Horder holds, should be responsible for the health of 4,000 patients. "That may be making medicine available for every citizen, but is it medicine?" he asks.

One well-known surgeon, Scott Edward, bases his opposition on a different argument. "As a surgeon visiting a hospital today," he wrote recently, "I take responsibilities for human life and happiness, for hope or for despair, success or failure, life or death for 15 shillings (about $3) each."

This sort of injustice, however, is being recognized, and payment for specialists is going to be reconsidered. It is one of the quirks that were inevitable in starting anything so colossally new as the National Health Service. Lots of doctors are grumbling, but in the nature of things it is the grumblers whom one hears and not those who are quietly and determinedly trying to make the scheme work.

It will be years before there are enough dentists, enough nurses and health visitors, enough hospitals and beds, and above all, before the "health centers" that will form the real basis for service in the future are built. Success of the whole health act really depends on these centers, where doctors, specialists, nurses and clerical staffs will all work together, sharing expensive equipment and laboratories and handling their patients with maximum speed and efficiency.

Meanwhile, if the National Health Service is working smoothly in ten years, it will have been a great accomplishment. And there will be no turning back even if the Conservatives win the next general election, partly because eggs that are scrambled can't be unscrambled, and partly because everyone applauds the ideal behind the new service. Critics have no valid alternative to offer, which was why the British Medical Association finally agreed to cooperate with the scheme.

If the Tories come back to power they will make changes in the health service, but they won't try to abolish it. A great social experiment is under way, and a nation is committed to make it work.

Part 3

YEARS OF REAPPRAISAL, 1951–1970

WHILE THE Welfare State was built—a task which the nation, with good reason, entrusted to the Labour party—Great Britain entered an era of national reappraisal. There were those, Churchill foremost among them, who held that her victory in war had restored Britain's role in the world; others countered that such success would prove as delusive as had the Versailles settlement. Thus Britain, uncertain of her position between America and the Soviet Union, divided as well over the ultimate fate of the British Empire, turned inward: her people were more concerned with the lot of the individual—in a basic sense, secure as never before—than with the destiny of the nation. Nor could Britain's leaders reverse this tide. Attlee's policies moved with it; his peacetime successor, Churchill, while adept in the conduct of foreign policy, was no longer the robust war leader and made little imprint upon domestic developments. Fifteen years after Churchill's resignation in 1955, Harold Wilson's Labour party may well have lost a general election because the electorate was concerned, above all else, with inflation's threat to the family. In the interim, and not coincidentally, the most successful politician by far was Harold Macmillan, who grasped the political rewards of untrammeled prosperity.

Macmillan had come to the fore at precisely the historical moment when the nation had recognized that her primacy in world affairs had vanished. Condemned by the United Nations and her erstwhile ally, the United States, for the Suez military expedition, Britain's near-isolation had been dramatically revealed. What may have penetrated even deeper into the national psyche was Britain's inability to sustain intervention at Suez in the face of U.S. opposition, while at the same time the Soviet Union went its own way in Hungary. The contrast was vivid, the lesson learned by all but a few. With this unmasking of British pretensions to world power, described by Barbara Ward, went the opportunity to make a new assessment of the United Kingdom's position. How well Macmillan utilized that opportunity is debatable. What is beyond dispute is that Britain, after the unmourned years of austerity under Socialist rule, grew more self-indulgent during Macmillan's regime.

In 1960 an English journalist, Charles Hussey, perceptively pointed out that a hierarchical social order had survived the leveling thrust of the Welfare State. Further, social institutions braked the pace of change; in the case of the elitist educational system—now, as then, very much in evidence—change was actually retarded. Much is made of the British workingman's refusal to put national interest above personal gain; the student of contemporary England would do well to counterbalance this with the persistence of class distinctions, and social privileges, within the framework of the Welfare State. At the same time, Americans ought not regard as a compliment to their way of life the alleged "Americanization" of Britain in these years, for what has been involved is the infusion of materialism and consumerism. Macmillan deftly incorporated both into the notion of Britain's never having had it so good, with the result in 1959 that the same could be said of the size of his parliamentary majority.

Possibly the key to understanding the political impact of Britain's rapidly changing social scene lies in the blurring of middle-class and working-class income patterns—"the upgrading of most working-class incomes into a vast, entrenched (but overspending), new middle-class Britain," in the words of the anonymous contributor to this section. But ideals did not succumb entirely to materialist pursuits. Edward Crankshaw, a prolific English journalist and historian, saw idealistic impulses motivating the protest movement of the early 1960's; in valuing even "ignorant, irrelevant and silly questions" of the mainly youthful protesters above blind acceptance of the assertions of politicians, scientists, and generals, Crankshaw recognized the age-old role of doubt in perceiving truth. His thoughtful essay makes clear that questioning dissent can be well-informed, relevant, and occasionally wise.

Though in 1948 Barbara Ward had pointed out the necessity for Britain's "taking the lead in a new economic pattern in Western Europe," the nation's governments, Labour and Tory, directed their reappraisals of Britain's role elsewhere. Far from captaining the new vessel, they missed the boat. Following the signature of the Treaty of Rome in 1957 and the establishment of the European Economic Community, Britain could hope for admission only on terms agreeable to the six Common Market countries. Macmillan's government attempted to minimize the demands made upon England, once negotiations were undertaken in 1961, but it could not avoid touching several sensitive nerves in the domestic body politic. These problems were well summarized in several *New York Times* articles (Charles Hussey, "Britain Stages a Great Debate," October 15, 1961; Drew Middleton, "Common Market and the Commonwealth," February 18, 1962); the most informative was written by Eric Johnston, a well-known American businessman. Though he undervalued the strength of Commonwealth ties felt within the governing Conservative party, Johnston built his case on economic factors. For his rather more important part, Charles de Gaulle based his veto of British entry upon his belief that Britain had not broken away from dependence upon America. Seven years later, in 1970, the question of British entry is again at center stage; in the interim, the Labour party has opted, conditionally, for entry. Once again the opposition party, Labour may reverse that stand, as its industrial backbone, the Trades Union Congress, sees several objections to membership. Since the TUC has recently acted as the tail that wags the dog, Labour conceivably might make a political issue of the Common Market. Even lacking that development, inclusion in Europe's "new economic pattern" bodes well to be the basic question in the reappraisal of Britain's role in the world of the 1970's.

As Prime Minister since June 1970, Edward Heath is no longer the "Tory outsider" about whom Anthony Lewis wrote in 1966. Along with the then "Labour insider," Harold Wilson, Heath will likely dominate British politics well into this decade, since both men are only now in their mid-fifties. Lewis' dislike for the Labour leader is quite apparent, despite Wilson's undoubted success in governing with a small parliamentary majority. His personal triumph in 1966 strengthened his hand, but fiscal setbacks, culminating in a devaluation of the pound which Wilson resisted to the bitter end, plagued his government. Having once assumed credit in overgenerous measure, Wilson could not divest himself of subsequent blame: such is one consequence of the "presidential" system of government which Wilson openly conducted in England. In seeking historical perspective on Harold Wilson's style of government, one inevitably recalls Lloyd George; whether either was the "illusionist without ideals" (Iain Macleod's withering criticism of the Labour leader) seen by his political foes, both relied upon parliamentary successes—call it "magic" or sleight-of-hand—to consolidate their position. Interestingly, Anthony Lewis' dislike of Wilson had by 1970 deepened to the point of hostility ("All's Right with the World of Harold Wilson," *New York Times Magazine,* June 14, 1970), though along with many seasoned political correspondents, and in company with Wilson himself, he failed to see that appearances, and pre-election polls, were deceiving.

Now Britain's Agonizing Reappraisal

by Barbara Ward

LONDON

THE FIRST task Prime Minister Macmillan and his Ministers need to undertake is to lessen the British people's sense of utter confusion.

There is a general awareness that a crisis has occurred in the country's fortunes. But no two people agree on its nature. Was the Suez intervention justified and wrecked only by American opposition? Or has Britain behaved outrageously and invited world denunciation? Has the British economy sustained a fatal blow? Or is petrol rationing barely necessary? Will things get much better? Or much worse?

The weeks of uncertainty between Sir Anthony Eden's return from Jamaica and his resignation only increased the popular bewilderment.

During that time, there was virtually no guidance whatsoever for public opinion by official sources. What there was seemed to make matters more confused. The outlook for petrol rationing, for instance, changed from statement to statement. If the mood

From the *New York Times Magazine,* January 20, 1957, copyright © 1957 by The New York Times Company.

of the country when Mr. Macmillan took office could be summed up in a word, it was one of apprehension.

This aroused state of opinion can be Mr. Macmillan's opportunity. One of the greatest difficulties facing British statesmen since 1945 has been that, while conditions have again and again been extremely precarious, the majority of Britons have "never had it so good." The fuel crisis of 1947, the devaluation of 1949, Korea in 1950, renewed economic crisis in 1955 all occurred against a background of uninterrupted employment and expanded welfare. The leaders might talk of crisis. The electorate filled in coupons for the football pools.

But the Suez débâcle seems to have broken through the crust of contentment—or apathy. It may create a demand for leadership and by so doing enable Britain's continuing crisis to be explored and countered.

Fundamentally, it is the same crisis. The vital questions about Britain's post-war policy and position are still unanswered more than a decade after the end of the war. Internally, the economy is still overstrained to the point of inflation. In spite of really important capital expansion in the last three years—of the order of £1,500,000,000—demand has kept ahead of supply; demand in the shape of social services, a defense effort absorbing more than 8 per cent of national income, capital funds for overseas territories and industrial expansion at home. The pound, falling 2 per cent in the last two years alone, is now worth not much more than a third of its pre-war value.

The workers have kept ahead of this devaluation. Their standards are perhaps 20 per cent above the 1939 level. But most salaried and white-collar employes have seen their income fall by half. Their frustration is becoming apparent. At elections, they stage the "stay-in strikes" of Conservative voters. They provide some of the lengthening queues before Commonwealth immigration offices—there are six times as many would-be emigrants as before the Suez crisis. Their mood is giving an angry edge to some forms of writing and journalism. To many, the national humiliation of Suez seems the last straw.

It is all the more bitter for its direct connection with the second problem in Britain's continuing crisis—the passing of her predominant world power and the painful process of adaptation to second-class status, at least in terms of strength.

Since 1945, it has been a fact that Britain cannot "go it alone." But the fact was not exposed in utter nakedness before Suez. The passing of power has been veiled in generalities—in Atlantic unity, in European cooperation, in the Commonwealth family, in the United Nations association. Below these broad terms, Britain, in fact, worked to maintain an independent policy.

The British Government has, in the eyes of its partners, usually been less than wholehearted in its cooperation with any of these possible groupings. The last decade echoes with complaints that London has been "dragging its feet" or playing one association off against another, pleading a special European position to avoid Commonwealth commitments and the Commonwealth position to strengthen a separate hand in Washington or Strasbourg or Bonn.

But, in a sense, these maneuverings reflected lack of certainty springing from a lack of power. There is no exercise more testing to dignity and good sense than the passing of authority. The temptation is to evade the issue. After Suez, this is no longer possible. A new assessment must be made.

The suggestion before the new Cabinet is this—whether the doubt, the bewilderment and anger aroused by Suez can be mobilized behind a real attempt to meet Britain's fundamental need for new policies, or whether the mood will be allowed to turn in upon itself in resentment, cynicism and bitterness. If ever there was a challenge to leadership, it is provided by the Suez aftermath; but, so far, it is only possible to say that the opportunity exists, not whether it will in fact be seized.

At home, the problem is, above all, the need for a new spirit in industry. The massive investment of the last three years provides the technical background; the British economy can probably afford wage increases of about 3 per cent a year. What it cannot afford is a situation in which productivity rises by 10 per cent both in Britain and among her German and American competitors but their wage bill rises by only 10 per cent and Britain's by 20. Present signs are that the trade unions, faced by patchy unemployment and short-time working, which post-Suez dislocations may aggravate, are in a more moderate mood. If their demands can be held to a 3 per cent—not a 9 per cent—increase one great section of the dike against inflation will have been held.

But the negative task of checking excessive wage demands is only half the battle. The positive need is a restoration of drive, adventurousness, incentive and opportunity at every level in the economy. This is the daily theme of public controversy. The country is not short of the basic materials—brains, character, discipline. Inventions are made, industrial innovations carried through. Hardly an industry is without some pioneer establishment, some model firm. But spirit cannot, apparently, be generalized.

Conservatives and Liberals believe that the chief fetter is excessive taxation and that economic reward is the best incentive for enterprise. The Labor party, committed to equality as a major political aim, cannot agree but is no longer certain of any alternative.

The issue was beginning to reach the center of national debate even before Suez; but the post-Suez atmosphere will probably not be favorable for experimenting with the Conservatives' thesis. Petrol rationing, the interruption of cargoes through the canal, higher freight rates, declining production in petrol-starved Europe, all threaten a year of reduced industrial activity and wider unemployment. It would be an electoral gamble to relieve the middle class at a time when some workers were facing the dole for the first time.

Mr. Macmillan has even spoken of higher taxation to cover the cost of Suez. Yet, provided their ranks hold together, the Conservatives need not face an election until 1959. If, by that time, the effect of marrying tax relief to productivity and enterprise had shown results in higher prosperity, the Conservatives might not lose. They would at least recover the stay-at-home voter whose absence has jolted them in all recent "safe" by-elections.

The verdict so far must be that the economic dislocations of the Suez crisis are more likely to make the negative contribution of slowing down wage increases than to achieve positive results in greater incentives to earn and produce. But it is difficult to consider the possibility of tax relief in Britain, as a contribution to domestic solvency, apart from the overriding problems of post-Suez foreign policy.

Suez has only underlined what was already fact—the strain of Britain's overseas commitments. The annual defense expenditure of £1,500,000,000 is the largest single unproductive drain on British output, and despite an expenditure of some £7,000,-000,000 in the last five years the whole handling of the Suez intervention suggested a defense establishment still unfitted to its task.

The fact that Western Germany spends proportionately half as much on defense is a relevant factor in German economic competition. The Belgian and French proportions are also smaller. And Britain, unlike these states, has to spend her NATO contribution in foreign currency.

Moreover, in the last eighteen months, the bases which were supposed to add to the Free World's security—in Cyprus, in Singapore—have become centers of expensive disaffection. These were facts, no doubt, before Suez. Now they are becoming grievances.

There is, thus, danger that, in an angry aftermath to disaster, the reassessment of Britain's position in the world may be undertaken urgently but resentfully. The result could be disastrous both for the British and for their associates. The temptation is strong to slash defense expenditure one-sidedly, to cut down British contingents in Europe, even to remove them altogether. Britain would as a result not only weaken the Western powers' European base but it would also throw away essential bargaining counters in the West's search for a balanced disarmament agreement with Russia. At the same time, France and Germany might well revive their old phobias in the light of British withdrawal.

Outside Europe, the British could be tempted to abandon their expensive attempts to underpin security in Malaya and the Indian Ocean. Their reappraisal, in short, could take the form of a real attempt at isolationism, a real turning of the British back upon external responsibility, a new "Little Englandism" at whatever cost.

And it is unhappily true to say that one universal strand in the present British mood—the strand of violent anti-American feeling—encourages such sterile and resentful reasonings.

"If the Yanks want to stop communism, they can go and do it themselves." In that reaction, the Grand Alliance dies. Yet it is a frighteningly general reaction in Britain today.

The Suez crisis has stirred up this mood, bringing to the surface all the latent resentment felt by Britons who have seen their authority superseded by the younger, stronger American nation. But there is at least a hope that the outcome of the crisis will prevent these useless emotions from setting the course of British policy toward embittered isolationism. For, however much the shock of Suez may encourage the British, an insular people, to "stand on their own," no conceivable crisis could have shown them more conclusively that isolationism is impossible.

Among all the other naked facts which Suez has bared is the utter dependence of Britain and Western Europe upon Middle Eastern oil. There can be brave talk of atomic energy. The fact remains that all Britain's plans for future expansion, all hopes of doubling the standard of living in the next twenty-five years, all aspirations for a better, fuller life for all classes and for a self-respecting foreign policy, depend upon the certainty of 40,-000,000 tons of oil a year by 1965. This figure assumes virtually a doubling of existing plans for nuclear energy. It assumes the highest conceivable rate of coal extraction. Yet the absolute dependence remains.

Nor is Western Europe in much better case. This is why the irrational Arabs, egged on by the coldly rational Russians, hold a knife at Europe's jugular vein. Suez has simply shown that unilateral British action sharpens the knife. It can be removed only by the closest, most detailed and sustained cooperation between Britain, Western Europe and the United States.

Britain and Western Europe, acting in absolute unity as oil users, can hope to extract some worth-while guarantees from the oil producers of the Middle East and can concert a capital program of constructing big tankers and alternative pipelines to end their dependence upon the Syrian and Egyptian channels. But to do this, they need the guarantee at once that they can, in the meantime, and if the Arabs are dilatory, receive oil from the New World without exhausting their dollar reserves. In other words, any concerted European scheme will fail without complete American support.

So long as Britain and Western Europe and America attempt separately to overcome the crisis thrust on them by Europe's total dependence upon Middle Eastern oil—a crisis of which Suez is one unhappy symptom—only the Nassers of the Middle East and the Khrushchevs of Russia will benefit. But a concerted plan deprives both Russia and the recalcitrant Arabs of their trump card.

Rightly interpreted, therefore, the Suez crisis could lead to closer and more integrated Atlantic policies, to clearer, more confident inter-Allied relationships and to a strengthening of the Free World's common front. Instead of sinking into embittered isolationism, the British have a chance to turn toward genuine European and Atlantic cooperation as a solution to the passing of their once-paramount power.

Yet this is an outcome which lies only partly within Mr. Macmillan's grasp. He can perhaps rally Western Europe to a common front. He cannot give the lead to Washington.

There, apparently, it is still not realized that Western Europe's dependence upon Middle Eastern oil is as paralyzing to its effective partnership in the Free World as was the threat of starvation in food and fuel that brought forth the Marshall Plan in 1947. Without oil, there can be no Atlantic Alliance, no strong Western Europe, no British outpost of freedom. This is the real issue which Suez has brought to light and the tragedy may turn to benefit if the crucial fact is realized in time.

In Britain, the U's
Still Have It

by Charles Hussey

WHEN Prime Minister Macmillan talks about increasing class-lessness in Britain and the end of class war, he is describing trends, not accomplished facts. For the truth is that there are still more class distinctions in Britain than in any other industrial democracy. In the age of the hydrogen bomb, the ghost of William the Conqueror strides the land. Tennyson said that kind hearts are more than coronets and simple faith than Norman blood—but it is still an advantage in Britain to possess noble ancestors.

Essentially—though there is more equality than there used to be and rather more possibility of moving up in society (with a resultant decrease in the gaps between classes)—the class system remains what it was at the beginning of the century.

At the top is an aristocracy that is continually being reinforced by the ennoblement of men of power and eminence. Next comes a ruling upper middle class, which still consists largely, though today by no means wholly, of people who were educated in independent schools outside the state system. Then there is a large business and professional middle class, very mixed in origin and social background, which in turn is supported by a widening lower middle class of clerks, small-time administrators and technicians who serve an expanding industry. Finally, there is a working class that is steadily shrinking as machines take over more and more of the tasks once done exclusively by manual effort.

Out of a population of about 37 million over the age of 16, approximately 25 million Britons might be designated "working-class," 6½ million lower middle class, 5 million plain and unmodified middle class, and something like a half million "top-level"—that is, in the upper middle class and aristocracy.

Of course, this is to divide the nation into its broadest categories. In Britain there are infinite variations of social class. Many people feel that their neighbors across the street are either low common folk or a bunch of stuck-up snobs. The class system of Britain is less a five-layer cake than a *mille-feuille* pastry—a pastry, moreover, that is being squashed in an age of mass-oriented mass production which is making us all more nearly equal in at least one important respect—as consumers.

One thing that helps to preserve the rigidity of the class structure: the old English love of a lord. Thus, the aristocracy, which has lost almost all its power, preserves a good deal of influence by its ability to dispense social patronage.

Another important factor that gives strength to the aristocracy is that honors and titles are still the supreme reward for social and political service. There is a nicely graduated scale of honors that starts with being a Member of the British Empire—a distinction that might be given to a diligent engineer of long service in the B. B. C.—and effectively ends with an earldom.

In this tradition-bound country, Clement Attlee, the former Socialist Prime Minister, is finishing his career as Earl Attlee. His deputy, Herbert Morrison, the son of a policeman and a parlor maid, has recently become the Baron Morrison of Lambeth —a seedy part of London that gave its name to the cockney dance, the Lambeth Walk.

All these merited rewards perpetuate class distinctions. The new peers bask in the reflected glory of the old nobility, and the nobility acquires new dignity by the constant addition of men of achievement. In this way, while rapid changes are taking place in British society, they are taking place *inside* the existing structure.

Most people would group the upper middle classes with the aristocracy, since they have so many important characteristics in common. They go to the same schools and universities, are members of the same exclusive clubs in the Pall Mall district of London, and speak in the same accents and with a common special vocabulary.

What binds them together most firmly is the common experiences of childhood and youth. When the time has come to leave Nanny at about the age of 8, they go to a preparatory boarding school and get grounded in Latin. About the age of 13, they go to a limited number of "public" boarding schools until they are 18, and then to one of two universities, Oxford or Cambridge.

This is not merely an education. It is vocational training for the exercise of responsibility and authority in a gentlemanly but very firm way. The public schools are training establishments to provide Britain with members of Parliament, judges, bishops, generals, civil servants and diplomats—and in recent years top management. For in Britain, as in the United States, the suave organization man is more suited to the great corporation than the old-style, aggressive, go-getting tycoon.

It is, however, in government that the upper classes largely preserve their influence. The Tory benches of the House of Commons are full of men who went to public schools. No fewer than seventy of them went to the same school—Eton—and seven Etonians, including the Prime Minister, are in the Cabinet. Labor has its public school men, too, headed by Hugh Gaitskell, the Labor leader, who went to Winchester.

Britons trained at prep and public schools, are, by and large, high-minded, industrious and public-spirited, and appear secure in any kind of society. Their defects are a lack of warmth and spontaneity. Not all of them are rich, by any means. Often their homes are shabby, but always in a distinguished way— chintz curtains, oriental rugs, antique furniture and real pictures on the walls. The radio is often pre-war and very low-fi. Unless they work in the City of London as stockbrokers, bankers, lawyers or high executives, they are careful to avoid dressing with glossy smartness.

The most important mark of their class is their speech. Few people who did not have this special kind of education can imitate its elegant glissando intonations without error for any length of time. One of the characteristics of upper-class vocabulary is to call a spade a spade and avoid face-saving euphemisms.

Upper-class speech was analyzed a few years ago by Prof. Alan Ross of Birmingham University, with some help from Miss Nancy Mitford, the aristocratic lady who writes pungent novels about high society. Ross' findings shook middle-class suburbanites who discovered that their refinements were not those of high society but quite the reverse.

For convenience, Ross called upper-class customs "U" and other customs "non-U." It seems that U-speakers do not call a chamber pot an "article," but simply a "pot." When they belch, they do not say "pardon"; they say nothing. And when they fail to hear, they simply say, "What?" In fact, in many ways, the upper classes share the blunt outspokenness of the working classes.

But, though the classes remain, their way of life is not what it used to be. There are peers of Parliament who do not own the robes they stand up in as they take the oath before the Woolsack, and baronets may pace the lawns of Buckingham Palace garden parties in gray toppers and morning suits hired from Moss Bros. of Covent Garden.

That the palatial life the aristocracy of Britain lived until 1914—and tried to restore in the Twenties and Thirties—is less opulent today than it used to be is only partly due to high taxation, death duties and inflation. Most of the nobility have ridden the financial storms pretty well with prudent investment policies and highly legal systems of tax avoidance based on the convenient fact that, though income is savagely taxed in Britain, capital goes scot-free.

The old life of leisure and pleasure has been hit more by the shortage of servants than by the shortage of money. The servants were conscripted for industrial and military service in 1940 and 1941 and most of them did not return to domestic service. In addition, they discouraged their children from becoming servants.

But there has been a change of tastes, too. The rich prefer comfort to luxury. Milord and his lady would rather live today in one cozy wing of the old house, or even in a centrally heated coachhouse, than sit at night in a cavernous hall with roaring logs at one end and icicles at the other.

Country house life still goes on, of course. The guns still bang at pheasant and grouse and 200 packs of hounds are chasing the fox. There are, however, many Masters of Fox Hounds who cannot take on the sole financial responsibility for hounds, kennels and hunt servants. Very often the hunt of today is run by a committee, which raises expenses from ordinary members.

In London, as in the country, there is a tremendous amount of gaiety and entertainment, but it is almost all professionalized or institutionalized, since none of the great town houses are still kept up. Though private dances are given for debutantes, most of the balls are held in hotels to raise money for charity. Dinner parties are small and intimate since even the wealthiest people usually live in small houses and flats. Nevertheless, "society" is expanding just now, because Britain is growing increasingly wealthy.

Because "society" is being invaded by successful and shrewd people, the society magazines have had to give themselves a new look and provide intelligent criticism of the arts. Paragraphs still appear, though, which seem to belong to the age of "Lady Windermere's Fan." Mrs. Fulke Walwyn, The Tatler says, gave a children's party at the Hyde Park Hotel, for 2-year-old Jane, who is "a niece of that maestro of the turf, Sir Humphrey de Trafford." There were, it seems, films, merry-go-rounds and whistles. "Anne Beckwith-Smith was the champion whistle-blower but I thought Victoria and Claire de Trafford, daughters of Mr. and Mrs. Dermot de Trafford, ran her pretty close."

Still, it would be wrong to deduce from this that there is a leisured upper class remaining in London. Practically all men, no matter how rich or how ancient their lineage, have full-time jobs.

Our next category—the professional and business middle class

—is living well today, though less comfortably than it did before the war when even quite a modest household might have four servants. Now, any middle-class housewife with one whole-time helper thinks herself lucky.

The social life of the ordinary British business man is built around Freemasonry, the Rotary Club, the golf club. He rather likes living in a suburb and does not understand why the upper classes believe that life is impossible except in the center of London or in the remote countryside. He dresses carefully, and his wife also.

Their house, however, would not pass muster with the "U" folk—all those fitted carpets, the large-screen television, the three-piece chesterfield suite in the "lounge" (a word used by the upper classes only to refer to rooms in hotels and clubs).

In manner, the business man often is bluff and jolly—and less refined than his wife would like him to be. He is suspicious of a Parliament that seems to be dominated by the upper classes, intellectuals and representatives of workers. But if he is a member of his local Conservative association he often selects as a candidate a member of the upper classes who has business interests.

The lower middle classes of Britain tend to be tidy, frugal, withdrawn, homebound and half-educated. Often they spend too much on appearances and too little on solid nourishment. Their main social concern is to differentiate themselves from the common people. This is the class which runs advertisements saying, "Superior person seeks rooms in good district."

The strongest characteristic of the lower middle classes is— or was—their ability to postpone satisfactions. They would not spend until they had saved and they would not marry until they had enough to start a home. They are ambitious, dislike trade unions and seek to identify themselves with management.

The working classes are jollier, less provident, scornful of fine speech and manners, pretty solidly bound with their fellow-workers and suspicious of authority. They are unambitious for themselves—though not for their children—and do not esteem workers who are too eager for promotion.

They loathe sarcasm, which they regard as a boss' weapon,

but they have their own rich ironic humor and exercise it on all the social classes above-mentioned.

What are the forces making for change in this remarkable society? Sometimes, paradoxically, they are the same as those that are producing rigidity. Undoubtedly the strongest impact on society is being made by the developing British economy.

About three years ago this economy took off in an American direction; it began to mass-produce on such a scale that manufacturers had to regard all social classes and not just the higher-income groups as potential customers. This tendency was reinforced by the advent of commercial television, which brought to a public that had never even heard a radio commercial the high-powered selling techniques of the United States.

A boom began in consumer durables, stimulated by installment buying. The indebtedness carried by the average family is now about £50—twice as much as three years ago. There is a car for roughly every three-and-a-half families and in ten years there will probably be a car for every two. At the moment, however, British workers are more home-centered than they have ever been.

"For the first time in modern British history," said Dr. Mark Abrams in a recent B. B. C. talk, "the working-class home has become a place that is warm, comfortable, and able to provide its own fireside entertainment—in fact, pleasant to live in." The total effect is narrowing "a working-class way of life which is decreasingly concerned with activities outside the home or with values wider than those of the family."

What is happening is that the working classes are merging with the lower middle classes. In the new post-war housing estates that now comprise about one-eighth of the total housing of Britain the two classes live side by side, wearing the same good, classless, mass-produced clothes, eating the same packaged foods and sending their children to the same schools.

The net result of all this has been to make Britain more conservative. Working people often say today that all this talk about class is old-fashioned nonsense. Many people believe that the Labor party lost the general election last October because the prosperous young workers refused to vote for a party which has traditionally identified itself with the working class. Douglas Jay, a Socialist front-bench intellectual, went so far as to say, "You can't fight under the banner of a class that no longer exists."

Thus it seems that Britain, which once consisted of "haves" and "have nots," is now becoming—to use a term invented by an American professor—a nation of "haves" and "have mores."

But is the gap between the lower middle and the business and professional middle class also becoming smaller? The answer is yes, but not very swiftly. The pressures at this level of society come from Britain's increasingly democratic educational system, but they are not very strong because the system is not very democratic yet and will not be for a long time.

About one child in five goes to grammar school (a preparatory school for university) and if he has brains he can reach a university. If he has very good brains, he may even get to Oxford or Cambridge. Some of these "meritocrats" from humble homes go into business or the higher grades of the civil service and even the Tory party finds room for some of them.

Nevertheless, the state grammar schools and the provincial universities, though they educate people to occupy top positions, do little to equip them with the social skills regarded as essential by members of the old ruling class in whose hands the power of promotion very often lies.

Britain is still divided into two nations by an educational system in which the sons of most of the successful men go to "independent" schools and the sons of the less successful go to state schools. And at the state schools, as recent research has shown, the humbler the home a boy comes from the more likely it is that his natural ability will fade away as he reaches the age of 16.

One of the big questions before British society is whether the best jobs are going to be given to the people with the best minds or to those whose minds are not quite so good but whose manners and accents are impeccable. It is the belief that caste counts for more than brains in Britain that has produced the Angry Young Man school of writers which has done much in the past years to revive class consciousness among the young.

Another big question is whether Britain, with its growing

wealth, is going to try to give a first-class education to a larger proportion of its children. Six out of ten leave school and start work at the age of 15. Only 11 per cent reach the sixth form, which leads to university, and over a third of these are in the independent public schools. Finally, only 5 per cent go to a university.

Out of every million of population in the United States there are 16,670 university students, according to a UNESCO survey made two years ago. Out of every million people in Britain there are only 1,815 at university.

The English educational system is designed to discover and promote élites as early as possible. Even in the primary schools the classes are "streamed" according to ability and at the age of 8 a child in a slow stream has probably lost all chance of a higher education. Only the exceptional child in England (Scotland is another matter) stands a chance of getting the best education unless his parents can lay hands on the £4,000 needed to put him through the independent system.

All the weight of technological change is pushing Britain toward a more egalitarian society. Most of the social institutions are impeding change or, as in the case of the educational system, making sure that the change is a slow one.

The British people are on the march but the lead of tradition is in their boots.

Portrait of Britain
in the "Fat Years"

by An Anonymous Englishman

The British recently took a hard look at themselves after a decade of affluence. Given a mass of facts and statistics gathered by Government officials, an English newspaperman (who has to remain anonymous under the terms of his assignment) wrote a report for the British Cabinet on the effects of the nineteen-fifties —the "fat years"—upon a nation which, in the previous decade, had emerged victorious but exhausted from World War II, rebuilt its industries and surrounded itself with the cushions of the welfare state. The author here writes of what he found.

IN THE nineteen-fifties, the class-conscious British coalesced into an absorbent middle class, spread out from town centers into an ever-widening suburbia, incurred heavy personal debts to build new homes and equip them with the gadgets of modern life, probably grew rather less moral than before, were caught up in a gambling fever, and retained their national resilience.

This resilience showed strongly in the census taken in 1951, the first for 20 years (the war had broken the decennial series). It examined the nation after the worst years of economic depression, the ravages of the most terrible war in history, the building of a new kind of society and a great diminution in its standing in the world. And yet, after all that, the number of people in the United Kingdom, already one of the most densely populated areas of the world, had risen markedly. So had the birth rate.

By 1951, most of the towns and cities that had been fiercely bombed from the air contained more people than had lived there before the war. The working population stood at a much higher figure than in 1939. Unemployment was reduced to little more than 1 per cent. The people were living longer and more healthily, partly because of the National Health Service and better nutrition of children, and partly because of higher living and educational standards.

Ten years later, by the national census of 1961, the population had increased by a further 2.5 millions—in England and Wales there were 790 people to the square mile. Although the birth rate had dropped from the 1947 peak (the year of the "bulge": babies fathered by men who returned from war service in 1946), it began to rise again from 1955 onward, and is still rising. So is the life expectancy of each child.

Behind these population statistics lie two big migrations that took place during the decade of the fifties. Many hundreds of thousands of British Islanders emigrated to Commonwealth countries, chiefly to Canada and Australia. They were not driven out by poverty or lack of jobs. The largest number, about 230,000, left in 1957, one of the most prosperous years. They went because they wanted to.

During the same decade, a slightly larger number of people migrated *into* the British Isles, to produce a net population gain of some 97,000. The immigrants came mostly from Commonwealth countries, especially from the West Indies, and in some parts of west and south London and in a few big provincial cities there were ugly outbreaks of color strife—the first of any real seriousness in Britain. (In 1962, an Immigrants Act was passed to control the flow.) There was also the usual steady immigration from the Irish Republic.

With the immigrants came two waves of refugees—the British who were cast out of Egypt after Suez, and some 21,000 Hungarians fleeing from their collapsed revolution. In the past quarter-century, Britain has taken in the sad total—or, from another point of view, the *proud* total—of about 330,000 refugees, most of them from Europe. The majority are now fairly well integrated into the larger cities of the land.

The other big population movement in the fifties was far more subtle and, for Britain, far more important. It was an internal migration of people from all over the British Isles into a few overcrowded areas coupled with an outward expansion from large towns into neighboring villages and suburbs.

Ever since the nineteen-twenties, some 40 per cent of the British people have lived in seven big conurbations—around London, Manchester, Birmingham, Glasgow, Leeds, Liverpool and Newcastle-upon-Tyne. During the fifties, still more people moved from other parts of Britain into these areas. In particular, they trekked into the industrial midlands around Birmingham, and into the southeast corner of England that includes London.

The population of Greater London itself actually declined by 176,000 people, but that did not imply a migration from the capital. What happened was that families moved out from central London and its surrounding suburbs to a fringe of commuter towns and villages. They spilled clear across London's Green Belt (land safeguarded from building), spreading along every major road and rail route out of the city and well beyond the New Towns that were originally designed to take London's overspill. To encompass the whole population centered on London today, one must now envisage a rough circle with a radius extending some 40 to 50 miles from Piccadilly. This new greater London takes in Brighton on the Channel coast, and stretches north into the hitherto sleepy agricultural counties of East Anglia.

The same kind of migration is taking place from the inner areas of most of Britain's bigger cities. In fact, the most marked population increases during the fifties were in towns of between 50,000 and 100,000 inhabitants.

What is being established around London and elsewhere is a sprawling suburban life comparable to the American model and made possible by the motor car. This was the decade in which the British got motorized. In 1951, there were 2.5 million private cars on Britain's mostly twisting and narrow roads. In 1961, there were nearly 6 million. The estimate for 1970 is 15 million, by which stage the island's traffic may have choked to a halt.

The first effect of the new suburban sprawl around Britain's cities was to put most householders into long-term debt. The houses were mostly bought on mortgage, and equipped and furnished on the installment plan. Britons' credit debts more than doubled between 1955 and 1961—much of the borrowed money going into cars and household equipment. British housewives at last clamored for the mechanization they read about in advertisements. Three out of four now have a vacuum cleaner; two out of five, a washing machine, and one in three, a refrigerator. The number of television sets doubled between 1955 and 1959 (the period in which the second—commercial—channel opened up). By 1962, there were 12 million in use, representing eight out of 10 households. In the fifties, too, the number of telephones nearly doubled and the increase would have been greater still if the Post Office had been permitted to make the capital investment needed to meet the demand.

In one respect, the sprawling suburbia of Britain even outdoes that of the eastern United States. British commuters travel to work mostly by train—particularly into London, which has probably the most efficient and most overworked short-haul passenger railroad network in the world. The Southern Region alone of British Railways carries more passengers per day than all the leading railroads of the United States combined.

But the weight of traffic on many of the commuter routes now exceeds capacity, so that rush-hour punctuality has sadly decreased. A survey in 1954 showed that the average worker in central London spent rather more than one and one-half hours in daily travel. The time is certainly longer now. The wearing frustrations of rail commuting have probably been a considerable political factor also, and may well have contributed to the anti-Government, pro-Liberal revival in by-elections on the dormitory fringe.

Although unemployment figures rose sharply (one hopes, temporarily) to beyond the 800,000 mark in the winter of 1962-63, the previous decade as a whole produced a 1.5 million increase in the working population, even though many more young people were drawn off into universities and technical colleges. As a result, the gross national product rose by 30 per cent.

There were also vast changes in incomes. The total of personal incomes almost doubled during the decade, while retail prices in the shops increased by only 50 per cent. Consumption per head rose by a quarter, mostly from 1952 onward.

One result of rising incomes was a big upsurge of thrift. Personal savings rose from 2.5 per cent of disposable income in 1951, to 10.5 per cent in 1961—the total then standing at £2 billion ($5.6 billion). As people became better off, they also lost their timidity about investment. The Stock Exchange no longer seemed so remote and forbidding. Today, there are more than 3 million individual shareholders in Britain.

Income increases produced some fantastic shifts in social status. They were the mainspring of the movement of the British into the huge middle-class stratum. At the start of the decade, more than half of all incomes were at the working-class level of under $14 per week, after tax. Most of the rest were in the lower-middle-class range of between $14 and $28 per week. Only 3 million people had incomes above that figure, and most of those were earning less than $42 per week. Only 90,000 people had incomes higher than $112 per week, after tax.

By 1961, more than half the working population had moved into the $28–$112 per week income bracket (after tax), most of them into its upper reaches. The number of people with incomes after tax of more than $112 per week had better than quadrupled.

Some economists say that fringe benefits and tax evasion have created wider gaps than before between the new-rich and the middle class. One put it bitterly: "The Tory aim of a property-owning democracy has been converted into a property-developing plutocracy." That may be, but it does not affect the chief factor of the decade—the upgrading of most working-class incomes into a vast, entrenched (but overspending), new middle-class Britain.

In terms of money, there has been a similar blurring of old class distinctions between "blue-collar" factory operatives and "white-collar" office and shop workers. The wages of each are no longer very different. All the same, there has been a big switch from blue-collar to white-collar jobs. During the decade, the number of factory wage-earners increased by only 2 per cent while the number of salaried office workers rose by 34 per cent. More than a million extra jobs were taken up in the professions, insurance, banking and finance, and the distributive trades. The switch could turn out to be a timely preparation for a speed-up in the mechanization of industry.

Much of this, however, ought to be expressed in terms of "white-blouse" or "blue-overall" jobs. The married women of Britain, who before the war nearly all stayed home minding their families, have gone marching out to work. More than one-third of all workers in Britain's factories and offices are now women, and more than half of them are married. During the decade the number of married women in jobs rose by nearly 40 per cent.

The most remarkable increase was among middle-aged housewives whose children had grown up. They probably needed the extra money to keep up payments on their household gadgets, cars and television sets. Nearly half of all wives between 40 and 54 years of age now have jobs outside their homes. Some, of course, work only part-time, but if all the working wives gave up their jobs and went home, Britain's industry and commerce would be dislocated overnight.

The extra money they earned played a big part in the affluence of the fat years. British families are now spending one-fifth more on food (taking into account the changing value of money over the years). They are buying more meat, sugar, fruit, vegetables, beverages and manufactured foods—and less bread and cereals. (Working housewives are also dieting for their figures' sake.)

Some of the extra money went on buying luxury additions to the National Health Service. With the expansion of middle-class attitudes, there has been a rush to join provident institutions that, for an annual premium, pay part of the cost of private hospital rooms and surgeons of the patients' choice. In 1951, there were only 100,000 people covered by this kind of insurance. By 1962, there were 1,200,000.

Much of the family money has gone, of course, on the children.

They are better fed, bigger (14-year-olds are on the average half an inch taller and three to four pounds heavier than school children of the same age in 1950) and better educated. The number of children in state schools staying an extra (voluntary) year nearly trebled during the decade—though many could not then go on to a university for lack of places.

Most of the children upon whom so much is being lavished are growing into people very like their parents, but there has also been a horrifying jump in juvenile crime. At the start of the decade, young men convicted of serious crimes were already over-filling prisons and Borstal (reformatory) institutions. Around 1954, the crime situation improved and there were hopes that the postwar tide had turned. But, as the country grew more affluent, it came flooding in again. The most disturbing increases were in crimes of violence committed by boys under 17 years of age and young men under 21.

Social workers are convinced that, aside from crime, moral standards generally among young people have sharply declined— particularly standards of sexual morality, although this is difficult to prove statistically. The number of teen-age marriages greatly increased (the number of bridegrooms under 20 trebled) and one in three was a shot-gun marriage, forced by the girl's pregnancy. (This is only marginally higher, however, than the prewar percentage.) One in five of the teen-age marriages that took place since the mid-fifties has already ended in divorce.

The uneasy feeling is that the increase of crime and the lowering of moral standards among youngsters match a growing materialism among their parents. With larger incomes have come more expensive tastes. More than 3.5 million Britons now cross the Channel each year on Continental holidays—spending $756 million as against $235.2 million in 1950. Most London typists now reckon to get a week or two in Switzerland, Spain or Italy.

Other leisure spending has been inflated, too. Five million people go dancing every week (there is said to be more dancing in Britain now than in any other country). There are 19 million devoted British gardeners spending astronomical sums on plants, fertilizers and tools. Domestic pets have multiplied in startling numbers: 4 million dogs, 6 million cats and 9 million caged birds (one home in four now contains a bird in a cage). Large extra sums are spent on music (records), reading matter (books as well as newspapers and magazines), and what has become the national hobby of do-it-yourself home decorating and refurbishing.

Alongside the spending is a grasping after unearned wealth. The amount of gambling in Britain is stupendous. In 1961, the gambling turnover (on horses, dog-racing, and a sort of weekly football lottery called "the pools," in that order) was reckoned at $2.1 billion—$39 per head of the population. Since then, it is known to have risen sharply. After the Betting and Gaming Act was passed in 1960 to legalize forms of back-street gambling that were going on anyway, more than 10,000 betting offices and up to 100 night gambling clubs opened throughout the country in the first 12 months. In the same period, some $70 million was staked on bingo, much of it by housewives.

This picture of the British after an affluent decade was drawn when it was assumed that Britain would soon enter the European Common Market. As yet, it is too early to tell whether the country's exclusion from the Six will cut away the foundations upon which the new middle-class Britain has been built. But whatever happens, some of the trends are bound to continue.

Demographers say that the main population developments, including early marriage and early birth of the first child, are not firmly related to economic circumstances and will remain. The main social trends will persist. More people will want to move into an outer suburban life, buy cars, educate their children longer, suffer their surgical illnesses in private rooms at hospitals, spend evenings staring at television, spend more, gamble more, buy more washing machines on credit and take their holidays in Italy. But whether they will be able to do all or any of these things depends, of course, on a continuing high level of national prosperity.

If the fat years should be succeeded by lean, the only certain clue to the future to be drawn from the fifties would be that Britain will never relapse into the working-class poverty it knew in the thirties. It has become a nation of middle-class householders, far too deeply committed to a middle-class way of life to give up without a huge struggle. History has shown the British to be a resilient people, coming back strongly after periods of widespread change and intense stresses. It seems likely, therefore, that, whatever the circumstances meanwhile, the census of 1971 will tell a similar story.

Challenge from
the British

by Edward Crankshaw

LONDON

BRITAIN IS not going "soft" on communism; nor is she going back
on NATO. Any reports to the contrary can be dismissed out of
hand. She will play her part in the great alliance; but she needs
to know what that part is and what the alliance is for. She is in a
questioning mood; and she has every reason to be, seeing that her
own future as a habitable land is at stake.

The questioning is sometimes ignorant, sometimes irrelevant,
sometimes plain silly; but sometimes it is very much to the point.
I would prefer a nation to ask ignorant, irrelevant and silly questions than to ask none at all and to believe all it is told by its
politicians, scientists and generals—and by the politicians, scientists and generals of its allies.

Many of my American friends are disturbed by the amount of
marching up and down and sitting about on pavements now going
on in Britain in protest against "the bomb" in general and in particular against Americans and American installations based in
England as part of the Western defense system. Is there, they ask,

any future in trying to defend people who do not want to defend themselves? They tend, some of them, to link up these activities with what they believe to be the "appeasing" tendencies of British politicians and with the shortcomings of the British contribution to NATO. They discover a new spirit of pacifism at work, which worries them.

They forget, those who are old enough to remember, that they were worried by the same sort of thing in the Thirties, but that, when it came to a showdown, all the peace pledges and Oxford Union resolutions about not dying for King and Country did not prevent Britain challenging Hitler when it seemed, belatedly, the only thing to do.

In one sense, much too much fuss is being made about the "ban-the-bomb" movement in its various manifestations; in another sense not enough.

There are a number of points to get clear. The first is that although they make a great deal of very public noise the anti-bomb demonstrators are numerically very few. The second is that even these few are very much divided in their motives and their aims. The third and most important point is that there is a certain reluctant sympathy for the best of the demonstrators among increasingly large numbers of people who consider them wrongheaded. The reasons for this sympathy need to be understood: some of them could so easily be removed.

The anti-nuclear demonstrators are very far from being a compact and homogeneous body. They range from genuine pacifists to exhibitionists, from those who are moved wholly by moral revulsion to those who are simply frightened. They include many who are making a generalized protest against authority in specific terms.

There are a few Communists (by far the least important and significant element), rather more fellow-travelers, still more who are vaguely pro-Soviet—and, as such, anti-American. Some are anti-American without being pro-Soviet. Some are not anti-American at all, but simply anti-bomb. Some are simply questioners, who have moved past questioning to making assertions. These are the most interesting and significant, because they express in extreme form the mood of a very large number of Englishmen and women who are themselves asking questions and getting dusty answers.

There are not many out-and-out pacifists, but there are some. There always have been. They are the sort of people who, in past wars, have gone to prison or voluntarily exposed themselves to great danger as stretcher-bearers or fire-fighters rather than bear arms against their fellow men. I think they are wrongheaded, but admirable in their wrongheadedness.

They are not frightened people: they would rather be killed or maimed themselves than assist in the killing and maiming of others. They form a very small hard center in the anti-bomb movement. There is nothing to be said about them except that the world would be a poorer place if they were suppressed and that the society which refuses to allow them to exist is on the way to becoming a totalitarian society—as all societies in conditions of modern warfare do in fact tend to become.

These out-and-out pacifists are nowadays reinforced by a new and far more numerous element composed of those who are not pacifists in principle, who do not utterly reject the use of violence at all times and everywhere, but who draw the line at the killing and maiming of millions of civilians by remote control.

This is not an entirely new problem: There were plenty of people in the last war—and they included active combatants— who were revolted by the mass bombing of German cities; there were some who would rather have lost the war than win it by the destruction of Dresden and Hamburg—and Hiroshima.

The insane obscenity of nuclear warfare, which would not only kill and horribly maim millions but may also cripple future generations, has been the deciding factor which has moved thousands from distressed acquiescence in organized barbarism to active protest against it. In all human conduct a line has to be drawn somewhere (most of us, for example, draw the line at eating human flesh, or murder, or sleeping with our sisters: why?); and many people, in Britain and elsewhere, are now trying to draw the line at nuclear massacre.

They may or may not believe (some do; some don't) that the peace of the world, such as it is, has been preserved since 1945 first by the American monopoly of the atom bomb, then by the existence of the mutual deterrent; but they consider it wicked even to contemplate the use of such weapons, and they won't rest until they are outlawed.

These people are driven by their belief to advocate unilateral nuclear disarmament in its most extreme and its only logical form. They agitate not only for Britain's renunciation of the nuclear arm but also for her secession from NATO, so that she may renounce her dependence on the American nuclear arm.

They are moved not by fear but by horror and compassion. They know very well that by unilateral disarmament they would not be saving their own lives; since in a nuclear clash between America and Russia a neutral Britain could hardly hope to survive. But they would prefer to be blown to pieces, burnt up, poisoned or otherwise destroyed, or to be overrun by the Soviet Army, rather than defend themselves, or allow themselves to be defended, by methods which they consider wicked.

Like the total pacifists, they command our respect. There are not many of them. It seems that we need people like them to act as the conscience of the world. We should be in a very bad way indeed if there were nobody left to say, again and again, that it is wrong to contemplate, in the interests of personal survival, the slaughter and maiming of untold millions, even the destruction of this planet.

These two groups, the out-and-out pacifists, who reject violence of any kind, and the nuclear refusers, who reject the bomb for moral reasons, are the purists. They form a small minority among those who demonstrate against the bomb, themselves a very small minority of the total population of Britain. But they give a front of respectability and dignity to many who lack a high moral purpose but are simply angry or afraid, or both, and to the Communists and fellow-travelers, too.

Even so, in spite of the publicity they win for themselves in the press (largely as a result of the Government's somewhat ham-handed way of dealing with them) they are in themselves unimportant. Their real importance lies in the mood they represent, which, as I have said, is a mood of questioning.

The initials C. N. D. stand for the Campaign for Nuclear Disarmament, led by Canon Collins and first made famous by the Aldermaston March, a protest against the Government's nuclear policy in particular and the use of nuclear arms in general which has become an annual pilgrimage. It has been claimed C. N. D. has a million supporters, but this is the wildest exaggeration.

This figure is presumably arrived at by including all the members of those trade unions which voted against the official Labor policy on nuclear arms at the notorious Scarborough Conference in the autumn of 1960. In fact, these were not individual votes against the bomb as such; they represented the "bloc votes" at the disposal of certain trade-union leaders and the main purpose of this demonstration was an internal party matter having nothing to do with C. N. D. but with a ferocious onslaught on Mr. Gaitskell and the official Labor leadership.

The supporters of C. N. D. are few and far between; and these, the real activists, are themselves split in all directions, united only in abhorrence of nuclear warfare and dissatisfaction with the policies of the Conservative Government and the Labor Opposition. They are even formally split.

Lord Russell's Committee of 100, pledged to civil disobedience, has been repudiated by the C. N. D. leadership and remains a splinter movement, although, because of the photogenic nature of its activities and the personal distinction of Lord Russell, it is a widely publicized one. Comparatively few C. N. D. supporters believe in civil disobedience—i.e., refusing to obey the laws of the country—feeling that in a democracy the watchword must be persuasion and example and that people must fight for their ideas by constitutional means.

Many are skeptical about the soundness of Lord Russell's political judgment. He is indeed a grand old man, but they remember that this fighting philosopher, who went to prison for pacifism in the 1914 war and who now denounces as evil men all politicians who pin their faith to the nuclear deterrent, was scarcely more than a decade ago preaching a one-man crusade and demanding that the statesmen of the West should present Stalin with an ultimatum, telling him that he must either mend his ways or else be destroyed: that was when America still had a monopoly on the bomb.

. . . . . .

In 1959, Bertrand Russell was asked in a B.B.C. interview, a transcript of which was reprinted in this magazine: "Is it true . . . that in recent years you advocated that a preventive war might be made against communism, against Soviet Russia?" He replied:

"It's entirely true, and I don't repent of it. It was not inconsistent with what I think now. What I thought all along was that a nuclear war in which both sides had nuclear weapons would be an utter and absolute disaster. There was a time, just after the last war, when the Americans had a monopoly of nuclear weapons and offered to internationalize nuclear weapons by the Baruch proposal, and I thought this an extremely generous proposal on their part, one which it would be very desirable that the world should accept; not that I advocated a nuclear war, but I did think that great pressure should be put upon Russia to accept the Baruch proposal and I did think that if they continued to refuse it might be necessary actually to go to war.

"At that time nuclear weapons existed only on one side, and therefore the odds were the Russians would have given way. I thought they would, and I think still that that could have prevented the existence of two equal powers with these means of destruction, which is what is causing the terrible risk now."

. . . . . .

I mention this to show the confusion, or some of it, at the very top of the movement. Among the rank-and-file it is worse. Apart from the categories of out-and-out pacifists and nuclear refusers discussed above, apart from the Communists who support C. N. D. for their own disreputable reasons (these, of course, do not join in the protests against the Soviet tests, which have lately been a feature of the movement's activity), C. N. D. supporters are a very mixed lot indeed, ranging from young mothers afraid for their children, through all kinds and shades of humanitarians, to fierce young men at odds with the Government and the whole Establishment.

When I am asked what makes so many people in Britain appear to question a situation which is inescapable and to entertain dark suspicions of a policy which represents the best guarantee of peace that can at present be imagined—the policy of nuclear deterrence—I reply that in fact very few of them do question the policy as such, but, rather, the muddle which surrounds it.

There are very few who do not see in the deterrent, employed coolly and in the full knowledge of the issues at stake, a sort of hideous but inevitable insurance. There are very few who would really like to see the West throw all its nuclear armament into the sea and invite the Russians to do their worst. In this sense, apart from the demonstrators, who receive far more publicity than their numbers warrant, the British are fundamentally rock-steady.

But they ask that their political and military leaders, and those of their allies, should be rock-steady, too. And when they see some of these leaders and a part of the press of England and America saying things which suggest too much emotion and not enough thought, they are apt to get rattled and angry and to react in muddleheaded ways. This has nothing to do with pacifism or being soft on communism, but only with bewilderment, frustration and exasperation.

These emotions may be stimulated by all sorts of dissatisfactions. I cannot give an exhaustive list, but here are some specimens:

Britain's own insistence on making and possessing her own bomb, duplicating in what appears to be an insignificant way the American nuclear effort, instead of putting her own resources to more sensible use within the framework of NATO. Tied up with this is exasperation at the equivocations of Britain's defense policy.

The illiterate equation of Berlin with Munich, of negotiation with appeasement. Most people know, for example, that at Munich the British and French politicians were determined to give away some of Czechoslovakia and only sought the best means of doing so; they also know that the purpose of negotiations over Germany is the precise reverse of this: to convince the Russians that we shall not give way over West Berlin, and to start from that firm point.

The injudicious use of mindless slogans like "Better dead

than Red," which are irrelevant and silly—irrelevant because the antithesis is a false one, and silly because millions of Europeans of good character and proved courage in Poland, Czechoslovakia and elsewhere have shown that it is meaningless; they have chosen to continue alive under a passing phase of alien domination (as people all through history have constantly chosen) rather than destroy themselves.

Loose talk about the inevitability of war—a slogan which, having been dropped by the Russians, seems to have been appropriated by some Americans (who receive at least as much publicity as our own nuclear disarmers). Here it has to be remembered that the British know that they cannot escape total destruction if it comes to nuclear war. One does not have to be a pacifist to decide that a war which leads to the annihilation of one's country and all the people in it is not a war to be courted. Exhortations to mass suicide are not heroic, they are hysterical.

War has usually been regarded as the continuation of diplomacy by other means. The object of defensive diplomacy is the preservation of the people and the institutions of the state. If a war makes inevitable the destruction of the state and everybody in it, then clearly one has to think of other means of keeping the enemy at bay.

The recklessness of nuclear testing, whether French, British, American or Russian, which creates incalculable perils at a time when, to all appearances, both America and Russia have enough weapons in their stockpiles to destroy each other and perhaps the world.

To these, add a certain amount of anti-Americanism, fanned in the past by Mr. Dulles' brinkmanship and now by the General Walkers; a certain fear of Germany, the sources of which are obvious; a general distrust of politicians' platitudes.

These attitudes, which express themselves in passive bewilderment or in active revolt and bloody-mindedness, seem to me to be not unhealthy, though often muddleheaded. They are at least an indication that many people understand that the nuclear breakthrough has created a situation without precedent in history, to which past "solutions" offer little guidance.

This confused apprehension is the first necessary step toward dealing sensibly with the situation. When it is made abundantly clear that all responsible leaders in the West have understood the nature of their responsibility (at present some have not even begun to understand it), which is, quite simply, to preserve the institutions and the peoples of the West both from being over-run by the Russians and from the inevitable consequences of nuclear war, it will soon be apparent that the British, no less than their allies, are determined to defend themselves. They are, indeed—given a defense policy, firmly and coolly carried out, which really makes sense and which promises that a useful pur-pose will be served by whatever sacrifices they may be called upon to make.

Britain Ponders Her Most Complex Issue

by Eric Johnston

TO THE generally taciturn Britisher, the world these days is a noisy place. Voices in his Kingdom are raised in strenuous debate: to join or not to join the Common Market. This topic has generated more public discussion in Britain than any other since the war. And it has involved the present leadership in the most complex negotiations ever faced by any British Government.

The negotiations are expected to resume in Brussels early next month. Parliament will reconvene shortly thereafter. The debate will have to be resolved. Its resolution will profoundly influence the future not only of Great Britain but also of the United States and the rest of the world. Clearly, we have good reason to try for a deeper understanding of it. Above all, we need to explore its relevancy to us.

This is not easy to do at the moment. Avoiding the heat and absorbing the light of any debate is difficult. It becomes doubly so when we realize that the nerve ends of the British are probably more exposed now than at any time in the history of that stoic people.

In recent weeks I have talked with scores of Londoners. Out of these discussions with leaders of government, business, and labor came a welter of views and opinions, many of which tended to confuse rather than illuminate the real nature of the debate. Myriad special interests appeared to be using it as a forum in which to get a hearing for parochial, often irrelevant, positions. Few minds and fewer voices seemed centered on its hard core.

What are the key issues—the central questions that must be answered before the debate is resolved? At the risk of over-simplification, I believe there are three that dominate and will determine its outcome:

First, will entry into the Common Market give Britain what it needs to achieve greater economic growth?

Second, will the advantages of economic integration with Europe compensate Britain for the loss of its ties with the Commonwealth?

Third, will Britain's entry mean political unity with Europe and an undue loss of sovereignty and identity?

Consider the first—Britain's need for a more rapid rate of economic growth. Britain, like America, has been concerned about its slow rate of growth. The gross national product of both is rising at about half the rate of that of the Common Market countries collectively. In the longer view, total production in Britain over the last two decades rose only about 35 per cent. Compare this to the 129 per cent for the United States and about 120 per cent for Germany.

Why is this? Why should a nation as highly developed and with such industrial expertise as Britain fall behind? What is holding it back?

The British give many reasons. The majority blame the present state of the nation's industry which, they say, is engulfed by a lethargy that only drastic measures can dispel.

"British industry has lost its sense of risky courage," complained a financial editor. It is afraid to re-tool, modernize, and experiment, he went on. It is too reluctant to scrap old ideas and old methods.

A London banker put the problem in historical perspective: "In the past we were great innovators. The postage stamp, railways, time standards—Britain was first in all these. We did everything first. Now we do everything last."

There seemed to be general agreement that industrial productivity has fallen into disfavor. Some put much of the blame for this at the doorstep of the labor unions—to their power in concert with what is termed the "welfare state."

"The British worker now feels that leisure, status and welfare benefits are more important than productivity," said one businessman. "He forgets that you have to produce enough to pay for all these fine things."

But labor does not receive all the blame. "Where is our efficiency?" another industrialist asked. "Wages are three times higher in America, but the cost of building a hotel or motel in America is less than it is in Britain."

What these voices are saying is that British industry needs a healthy jolt, an incentive to stimulate industrial morale. A newspaper publisher had a more grandiose remedy: "We need to get into a competitive situation linked to a grand design and a great ideal."

If this is the case, then British industry does not have to search far. Competition and the grand design lie just across the channel in the Common Market. And in the minds of many Britons, there is no other long-range economic alternative.

As an illustration, three British trade unions recently completed a study of the motor-car industry. They concluded that entry into the Common Market is essential to the well-being of the auto industry in Britain. The report warns: "If we do not manage to integrate our trade with Europe within the next ten years, the demand for British cars will be so low that it would be impossible to continue producing them at prices which would compare favorably with cars we would import."

This attitude is in direct contrast to the sentiments of the many trade-union leaders whose major fear centers on the "free movement of workers" provision of the Treaty of Rome, the treaty signed by six nations—France, Italy, Germany, Belgium, the Netherlands and Luxembourg—which established the Common Market. Although surplus labor is drying up on the Continent, these labor chiefs insist that the immigration of European labor will have a ruinous effect on English jobs and wages.

Other foes of the Common Market frankly dispute the contention that entry will mean a faster rate of economic growth for Britain. They claim the mere formation of the Common Market did not cause Europe's growth, and point to other factors as being responsible. Among these are the influx of capital, the expansion of Europe's labor force due to the rise in the number of refugees, the Monnet Plan to re-equip French industry, and the economic aid that America gave Italy.

These, they say, were all there before the advent of the Common Market. From this, they conclude that Britain's entry is no guarantee that its economy will grow as did the economies of The Six.

Few, however, dispute the need for growth.

The second issue in the British debate is the problem of the Commonwealth.

The British are taking a dispassionate look at the Commonwealth. They are attempting to assess its real value and its potential in terms of Britain's present and future economic needs. They are not permitting tradition to obscure some facts that many would prefer not to face. Said a leading economist:

"Conditions aren't the same. The Commonwealth no longer has the significance it once had for both of us. The Commonwealth wants to industrialize, to become independent. In like fashion, modern technology is increasingly freeing Britain from the need for Commonwealth products such as butter and wool for which synthetic substitutes are available."

A Conservative M. P. said: "We've indulged in sentimentalism. After all, let's face it—the Commonwealth has little economic value to Britain."

He seems to have some salient economic statistics on his side. Between 1954 and 1961, United Kingdom exports to Western

Europe rose by 60 per cent and to the sterling area and Canada by 16 per cent. In the first four months of this year Britain's exports to Europe were, for the first time, higher than its exports to the Commonwealth. In this period 38.6 per cent of Britain's exports went to Western Europe while only 31.6 per cent went to the Commonwealth.

Clearly, the direction of British exports is changing. But many Common Market opponents contend that percentages do not tell the whole story. They prefer to cite the monetary value of the Commonwealth.

Consider, they argue, that Britain's exports to the Commonwealth run to about 1.4 billion pounds a year, while its exports to the Common Market amount to about 611 million pounds a year. They feel the British public is being misled when monetary value is ignored in favor of trends and percentages in the growth of trade. The Commonwealth, they contend, should not be sacrificed to dubious future economic advantages.

The British attribute the slower pace of their trade with the Commonwealth to four chief factors. First, general liberalization of trade during the 1950's has allowed other countries to break into Commonwealth markets. Second, the rapid rise in output of industrial Europe and Japan has led them to greater trade with the Commonwealth. Third, the weakness of commodity prices in a number of Commonwealth countries has cut their earnings and has lessened their ability to pay for imports. Finally, the pattern of economic aid to developing countries has diverted a growing share of international trade to North America.

An educator saw, in addition, a change in basic attitudes toward the Commonwealth. He summed it up: "There's a desire to be rid of the responsibility for the Commonwealth. And along with this, the feeling of community with Europe has increased."

A businessman took a stronger position: "Australia and Canada aren't so worried about saving Britain. In most items we're up against tremendous local protection throughout the Commonwealth." He gave examples, citing how the Canadian and Australian Governments did not consult Britain when they subsidized their ship-building industries to the detriment of British trading interests, and how, when Britain was finding it difficult to buy paper from Sweden, Canada took advantage of the situation and raised its prices.

Despite these apparent shifting attitudes toward the Commonwealth, few in Britain are calling for a break with no safeguards. They insist that a way that is both expedient and honorable can be devised to enter the Common Market.

Some see a possible solution in the proposal that the Common Market offer concessions to the Commonwealth for a limited period of time. As a Labor M. P. said: "These concessions cannot be permanent. Britain has every right to argue that the indefinite preservation of rights is unreal in this world."

On the whole, there seems to be widespread recognition by the British that the obstacles to entry presented by the Commonwealth will have to be surmounted. They feel it is neither in their own nor in the Commonwealth's best interests to turn away from the promising markets of Europe. A stronger Britain is in the best interest of all. A weaker Britain will benefit no one.

Edward Heath, Britain's Lord Privy Seal and its chief negotiator at Brussels, has said: "The work of constructive statesmanship should be to reconcile the new movements in Europe with the Commonwealth and all our ties with it to the enrichment of both."

The third issue in the British debate—and perhaps the thorniest of all—is the question of possible political unity with Europe and what this will mean to British sovereignty and tradition.

Much of the debate on this issue seems grounded in the past and the future to the exclusion of the realities of the present. Often overlooked is the fact that the Treaty of Rome does not irrevocably commit Britain to any form of political union, and, for that matter, does not contain any political provisions.

Nonetheless, old beliefs and future fears have a way of creeping into public issues. And they are not shed easily. The head of a university explained. "The city of London represents all things to us. It is here that we make decisions that control our country. But now Brussels? Unthinkable!"

Many British distrust the power held by the Common Market's High Commission in Brussels. Many are afraid that Parliament will become a rubber stamp. Because Britain has no written Constitution, many look upon the Treaty of Rome as a rigid, inflexible, and unnecessary document. Their impulse is to shrink from it.

Apprehension in this connection is voiced by Britain's Labor Party. Essentially, the Laborites are afraid they will be unable to carry out domestic social programs under the treaty. They make these points: The free movement of capital as envisaged in the treaty is incompatible with economic planning in the interests of the working people. The control of capital is necessary if economic planning is to be successful. The relinquishing of this control would make it impossible to plan for social progress and to reach social goals.

But Labor opposition has been much less than many anticipated. While the party is calling for safeguards on every front, it is not saying that Britain should not join. It is on the fence and is saying to the Conservative Government: "Show us the terms." Whether Labor will ultimately decide to turn away from the Common Market cannot be determined at the moment.

Many others, however, do not back away. One government official declared: "We must join the Common Market. Geography alone demands it. This country is a European country. We're the prodigal son, and it's about time we returned to the fold." He felt it was "error or wickedness" for opponents of the Common Market to suggest that Britain would accept commitments different from those agreed to by The Six. "Has de Gaulle surrendered any sovereignty?" he asked.

The supporters of the Common Market express the hope that the fear of closer political ties with Europe will vanish as the British come to know more about the goals and operation of the European Economic Community. They point to the outward-looking character of the E.E.C. as an argument for banishing what they feel are groundless fears.

To support this, they emphasize that the general level of the E.E.C.'s common tariff is lower than that of the United Kingdom's tariff. And, they give many examples of how the E.E.C. is evincing a sense of responsibility.

They point out that the Common Market nations are contributing some 20 per cent to the third five-year plan in India while Britain is contributing 11 per cent. To Pakistan's second five-year plan the E.E.C. is contributing 10 per cent, Britain 5 per cent.

Thus, the Common Market proponents argue, the record of the E.E.C. to date reflects maturity. This is a quality the British prize. As one Britisher said: "It all depends on how those chaps behave. If they behave sensibly, it will work out."

A substantial body of British leaders favors political unity with Europe. They believe that Britain can offer a great deal to the development of the E.E.C. They list Britain's political traditions and experience, and the stability of the British form of government. These things, they feel, would be benefits over and above the industrial strength that Britain would bring to the European movement.

I think the British writer, Roy Pryce, crystallized this in his new book, "The Political Future of the European Community." He wrote: "Perhaps it is not too much to hope that the Mother of Parliaments could again, as she has done in the past, provide a source of inspiration, as well as material help, for the construction of effective and responsible forms of government in the new Europe."

These three issues—the need for economic growth, the Commonwealth problem, and Anglo-European political unity—constitute, in my opinion, the crux of the British debate. I believe that if Britain can resolve this difficult trio, its entry into the Common Market will be accomplished.

For our part, I think we can draw much from the debate as it progresses. If we listen carefully, we may hear echoes of present and future debates in our own country:

Are we not looking to the new mass markets of Europe for a solution to our problem of economic growth?

Do we not have ties with Latin America, comparable in large measure to those Britain has with the Commonwealth, that cannot be ignored in any consideration of a closer association with the Common Market?

Isn't our political future bound up with the development of political unity among the free nations of Europe?

Unquestionably, the British debate is well worth our attention. For in listening we may find the elusive answers to some of our most complex problems.

The Labor Insider vs. the Tory Outsider

by Anthony Lewis

LONDON

IT IS A paradoxical choice that the voters of Britain face in the general election this Thursday.

The leader of one of the two great parties rides into battle carrying the faded banners of yesteryear's ideas, weighed down by tired rhetoric and tied to backward-looking interest groups. But he offers the assurance of an established presence and a masterfully comforting manner.

His opponent sounds the battle cry of radical reform, of death to vested interests, of experiment and break with imperial tradition. But he and his team suffer from seeming uneasy, edgy, untried—political outsiders.

The established figure is, of course, Harold Wilson, the Labor Prime Minister, and the outsider Edward Heath, leader of the Conservative party. And nothing, in the light of British political history, could be more paradoxical. For 50 years Labor has been the outsider, feared as dangerously radical and frustrated by the apparent acceptance of the Conservatives as the natural governors of Britain.

That things are in this topsy-turvy state can be attributed largely to the remarkable Mr. Wilson. In just 17 months as Prime Minister he has made what seems likely to be a lasting mark on British politics. He has given the Labor party credibility as a governing party and kept the usually secure Tories more or less continuously off balance. And the election campaign now almost concluded shows another notable contribution. He has hastened the transformation of elections here from contests between political philosophies to choices between two men.

Everyone likes to talk about how Britain is moving toward a presidential system. That can be exaggerated, in terms of both administration and politics. Responsibility for the functioning of the Government is still far from focused on one man to the extent that it is on the President of the United States. And in political campaigns there is little of the personal glorification that surrounds an American Presidential candidate—the bands, the buttons, the jumping girls, the shrieking crowds.

Yet it is clear that something is happening to the theory of British elections that good American boys and girls were taught in school. In that view, parties—not men—counted in the parliamentary system. In 630 constituencies all over these islands, the voters made their choices on philosophical grounds. Candidates were fungible characters who could, and did, run in any district, not necessarily home, and the party leader was just another one of the candidates. He was made Prime Minister, not by the voters, but by his party's members in Parliament.

Modern communications have changed that political theory. Radio and, even more, television have made the Prime Minister the center of interest, dramatizing the choice of leadership. Wilson, a nonideological figure, has encouraged a movement from ideas to personalities as the subject of elections by using television to reassure the middle class of his essential neutrality and respectability. Two-thirds of the voters are probably still committed to one party beyond persuasion. But for the vital last third, as the headlines and polls show, this election is, to a great extent, a race between Edward Heath and Harold Wilson.

The two men make a fascinating study in likes and contrasts. The similarities seem compelling—at first. Many Conservatives, in fact, thought they were choosing another Wilson when they made Heath leader last July. But time and reflection have shown the depth of the differences.

They are almost exactly the same age, Wilson having just turned 50 and Heath reaching that birthday in July. Their origins were about equally humble: Heath's father was a carpenter-builder, Wilson's an industrial chemist. Both went to state schools, to Oxford on scholarships, through economic training to the Civil Service and then politics. Their fathers both thought, so they say, that their boys would be Prime Minister some day.

As personalities, both are calculating-machine types. They seem almost afraid of genuine emotion, as if it had been burned out of them by ambition. Each is intensely ambitious. Each is a loner in politics, without the circle of friends and camp followers that a John Kennedy or Lyndon Johnson or Hugh Gaitskell had when he became leader of a party. But there the comparison stops.

Harold Wilson was born in the Colne Valley of Yorkshire, land of cold mills, black moors and bitter poverty—and of nonconformist religion and radical politics. His family never went through the starvation and degradation that rotted so many working-class families in the North in the nineteen-twenties and thirties, but that background still shows strongly in Wilson's social attitudes and tastes.

Society does not interest him. He hardly went out to dinner even before he became Prime Minister. As for inviting others in, he once asked an interviewer: "Why should I entertain if I don't enjoy it?" He belongs to no clubs and has never been seen in the brilliant salons of London.

In taste, his admirers describe him cheerfully as a Philistine—almost a compulsive one. His wife once joked publicly about his lavish use of H.P. Sauce, a thick, brown, spicy product that makes gourmets shudder. Asked about his reading, he said he liked Dorothy Sayers's "The Nine Tailors"—and had read it 15 or 20 times. Another time, he said he had been to see "Swan Lake" in Moscow 17 times. There is nothing square about Sayers or "Swan Lake," but, as Groucho Marx might say, who counts?

Private Eye, the satirical magazine, runs a biting feature on lower-middle-class life at 10 Downing Street called "Mrs. Wilson's Diary." One example, from an account of a Cabinet lunch: "We had prepared two large cauldrons of savoury mutton hash and two jumbo-sized syrup puddings, kindly supplied by the London Co-op. . . ."

No one would accuse Heath of Philistinism. He is, for one thing, an accomplished amateur musician. The Guardian observed recently that it was "revolutionary even to conceive of a Conservative Prime Minister whose idea of relaxation is not to reach for a gun and shoot something but to sit down at a piano and play Beethoven, Brahms or Schubert."

Another commentator remarked that he was "the first Tory leader to own a set of black leather Scandinavian armchairs." He lives in Albany, the superb 18th-century apartment house just off Piccadilly, in a chic duplex flat decorated in severe black-and-white modern but with paintings by Sargent, Augustus John and Winston Churchill. He belongs to two clubs. While Wilson still sounds the flat notes of his native Yorkshire, Heath's accent has become almost plummy upper-class, the main trace of his humble origin in Southeast England being an "ou"—as in "out"—sounded a bit like Southwest American.

An interesting difference between the two men appears in their attitudes toward each other. In private conversation, Heath reflects genuine distaste for Wilson—a view of him as a bounder. Heath's discussions of the Wilson Government are sprinkled with such words as "gimmickry," "disaster," "twisting," "flummery."

Wilson can be equally uncomplimentary in his public descriptions of the Opposition, but there does not seem to be any emotional distaste in his private attitudes. He views opponents as a biologist might view experimental mice.

Heath, on the floor of the House of Commons, becomes so irritated by Wilson that he cannot resist bounding up again and again to complain. The tactic is often unwise, because he gets chewed up by the master of parliamentary badinage, but the point is that his emotions are not completely throttled.

Wilson, by contrast, gave this answer when asked by a reporter how and why he controlled his feelings so tightly: "I have lost my temper a number of times, but I've usually known when I was doing it. It's a useful weapon. Occasionally, one has to play that particular card, but I think one is in a very weak position when you lose your temper without intending to do so."

Closely related to this difference in personality is a crucial point of political distinction—their commitment to issues.

There is no joy in examining the motives of politicians and weighing their relative "sincerity." The uncommitted man, the pragmatist, has his value in the system. Without carping, then, let it be said that Harold Wilson is completely that man. If he has any political philosophy or idea to which he is committed, objective students of his career have been unable to discover it. When it suited him to side with the left and fight Hugh Gaitskell for the party leadership, he did so. When, as Prime Minister, he wanted to reduce the left's influence, he did so. He can make a pledge of something specific like renationalizing steel more firmly and with less meaning than just about anyone else.

The favorable view of all this is that it works; Wilson has governed with a majority of three and kept a usually temperamental party in line. The unfavorable view was expressed as follows by the Conservatives' most pungent spokesman, Iain Macleod:

"John Fitzgerald Kennedy described himself in a brilliant phrase as an idealist without illusions. I would describe the Prime Minister as an illusionist without ideals."

Heath, whatever his motives, has built his political career on commitment to particular themes. The first—and still the deepest —is to British membership in the Common Market; Heath conducted the negotiations that ended with General de Gaulle's veto three years ago.

The belief that British industry needed to be toughened by stiffer competition was one argument for joining the Six. The same view led Heath, in the dying days of the last Conservative Administration, to introduce a bill wiping out retail price-fixing, the British equivalent of "fair trade." He drove it to enactment despite a major revolt within his own party.

Iron toughness in dealing with his own party has long been

a Heath characteristic. When he was chief whip at the time of the ill-starred Suez invasion, he had the job of bringing back into Tory unity both those who opposed the adventure altogether and those who thought Britain should not have given it up under American and United Nations pressure. The latter presented the harder problem, and he seems to have solved it by sheer brow-beating. A friend, checking a rumor, asked him in disbelief whether he had really called the Suez group "Fascists" to their faces. "No," he said, "I called them bloody Fascists."

The legislative battle over price-fixing left some personal resentment against him, and he admits now that he handled it too crudely, without enough preparatory discussion with his party colleagues. He has learned the lesson. Now he uses much more the Johnsonian technique of trying to achieve consensus before the battle—though not with the opposition party, a technique that the more partisan parliamentary system seems to exclude.

That he can operate smoothly and successfully was shown by his election as leader to succeed Sir Alec Douglas-Home last July. Few thought he could make it, but he turned out to have been working quietly among his colleagues for months, lining up votes.

When it comes to party management, though, the undisputed champion is Wilson. His technique is not Johnsonian, because consensus on particular programs is often impossible in the ideologically divided Labor party. Instead, he uses what could be called sleight of hand. When he dumps some cherished left-wing symbol, such as steel nationalization, he says solemnly that it is just "a matter of priorities," that steel will have its day. When the left attacks his support of American policy in Vietnam, he puts on a mournful face and suggests that he has gone without sleep for nights, worrying and telephoning in efforts to end this terrible war. Before the critics have time to wonder why he should telephone in the middle of the night, or for what purpose, the discussion in the House has turned to some other subject.

Wilson can be tough with his own backbenchers when he deems it wise. Last month, during a Vietnam debate in the Commons, he taunted his left-wing critics with really wanting not "peace" in Vietnam but "victory"—for the Communists. He said he would like to have seen the "peace in Vietnam" lobby parading, during President Johnson's peace offensive, "outside the Chinese Embassy."

But then, characteristically, he distracted his own backbenchers' attention from their attack on him. He charged that Conservatives had gone around, during a by-election campaign in Hull a few weeks before, urging voters to support a fringe left-wing candidate in an effort to beat Labor, and he called this "a mockery." The Labor benchers howled at the Opposition, forgetting their unhappiness over Vietnam in the joy of seeing Tory blood spilled.

Rallying his troops by such sallies at the Opposition is a regular Wilson technique in the House of Commons. Jokes and insults are his grist. A member from the county of Montgomery, in Wales, was attacking Labor one day for keeping forces east of Suez. Mr. Wilson popped up and retorted: "You know, you have an obsession about practically anything east of Montgomery." The laughter killed that serious discussion.

When Sir Alec was Conservative leader, he was the favorite Wilson target. A gentle soul, his discomfiture in the rowdy atmosphere of the Commons was distressing to see. Wilson picked on Sir Alec so savagely that even neutrals began to sympathize with him, but he got his own back last July 22, just a few hours before he announced his resignation as leader. Wilson answered a perfectly reasonable question from the Conservative leader by expressing the sarcastic wish that Sir Alec would "feel better" later. Sir Alec replied: "I sometimes wish that the Right Honorable Gentleman would behave like a Prime Minister."

The Wilson secret is that he *does* behave like a Prime Minister —outside the Commons cockpit. He well understands the difference between the audience there and the public audience on television. He is a savage politician in the first medium, a bland statesman in the second. On the screen, oleomargarine wouldn't melt in his mouth.

A Wilson television performance is a marvelous thing. Pipe in mouth, he ponders the great problems of world statecraft, sharing confidences with the viewers. He is serene and assured, even forgiving, under the sharpest questioning. Once a reporter criticized a television interviewer for not having pressed him hard enough. The TV man then played Wilson to the reporter's questions, ducking and evading and changing the subject with Wilsonian aplomb. The reporter retired in frustration after only a few minutes of the game.

Mastery of clichés is an important part of the technique. Wilson loves to say that Labor has provided "firm government," that it is unafraid to do "unpopular things," and ready to be "hard and tough." In a single television appearance in this election he used the words "courage," "guts," "honesty," "candor" and "frankness." His phrase "to speak frankly . . ." has been parodied by John Bird, a television satirist, to the point of becoming a national joke. But the frankness bit is not new. Six months before he became Prime Minister, an interviewer asked what he thought his faults were. He named three, and one was being too frank with the press.

Naturally, all this drives eggheads who are not Labor supporters to distraction. Watching one of his television performances is about as painful for them as watching Richard Nixon was for their American equivalents. An American viewer quipped the other night: "All he needs is a dog." The worst of it is that in private conversation—except possibly with a few intimates—Wilson is exactly the same, spouting the clichés about "firm government" and never showing the kind of wry detachment about himself that Kennedy had. He is like a Russian nesting doll; no matter how much you peel off, there is nothing to see but politician.

Labor supporters, just as expectably, find it all delightful. After a particularly flummoxing Wilson effort, an intellectual of Labor sympathies murmured in awe: "He's a genius. No. He's a saint."

The effect on the average viewer is the question that may be decisive this Thursday. The evidence to date is that the Wilson technique works. Partly, he inspires genuine confidence; he has given stature to his whole Government. There may also be a number of people who know that they are seeing a performance but enjoy it anyway, or think such artistry is what Britain needs now.

A middle-class housewife who was interviewed before the 1964 general election said: "I cannot bear Harold Wilson. He makes me grind my teeth. There is something about the man which is so thoroughly insincere. He is putting on an act all the time." The same housewife is now thinking of switching to Labor in this election.

Along with the bedside television manner, Wilson is a master of the public-relations technique of dominating the scene. During the Conservative party conference in Brighton last fall, he spoke to the nation about Rhodesia, visited the Queen and generally managed to keep Heath out of the headlines for days. John Bird parodied him in a mock broadcast that began: "Good evening. I have not spoken to you all since my emergency broadcast an hour and a half ago."

Finally, in this somewhat awestruck account of Wilson the performer, there must be recorded his tightrope act of survival for more than a year with a majority of three. He did it by a variety of changes of mood—exhortation, promises, accusation and statesmanship—that Iain Macleod characterized as follows:

"For the first 100 days the Prime Minister was a combination of John F. Kennedy and Napoleon. We had all this about decisive action. Then there was the Dunkirk spirit and the reincarnation of Winston Churchill. Then for a time—heaven help us— over Rhodesia he was Abraham Lincoln, with malice toward none and binding up the country's wounds. He emerged recently as the Duke of Wellington."

But the voter, again, may not see it as critically as Macleod. One keen observer suggests: "Wilson is running a puppet show, a magic act. The people know that well enough—they're not dumb. They just like it."

How does Ted Heath show up against the political skill of Harold Wilson? Until the election campaign opened at the beginning of this month, even Heath's friends would mostly have given a negative report. Over his first seven months as leader he had not provided the psychological uplift that the Tories wanted. He was clumsy and too thin-skinned in the House of Commons, and too boring outside. His speeches tended to be loaded with cold facts and statistics, with very little jam on the bread. On television, he seemed edgy and forced, with a Pepsodent grin that looked as though someone had told him a smile wins votes.

In the campaign he has distinctly improved. He has dropped the grin and become much more natural on television. He projects a quality of sincerity—that awful but inescapable word. His memory and his grasp of complicated facts are a match for Wilson's. He has impressed by his willingness to say bluntly things that are not calculated to win votes, such as that he will restore the nominal charge for prescriptions that Labor removed for National Health Service patients. He is blessedly less sententious than Wilson.

Nevertheless, he is not likely to win on personality points. He seems too cold, too remote, and he cannot put on the Wilson folksiness. "He lacks what the Elizabethans called 'nature,' " an acute Tory lady remarked—the quality of feeling for humanity. Women seem especially put off, either because of his crisp style or because they doubt the sexuality of a 49-year-old bachelor.

His admirers would say that any coldness projected by Heath reflects a steely quality that would make him a good Prime Minister, if not an ideal candidate. Certainly in conversation, private or at press conferences, he can give an impression of icy determination. At one briefing, he was asked how he would make railroad workers end featherbedding practices that successive Governments here, as in the United States, have failed to eliminate. He said crisply that there would be no wage increases on the railways, which are nationalized, until unions agreed to remove work restrictions. The questioner, slightly taken aback by his bluntness, said such a course would mean a national rail strike.

"That's right," Heath snapped, and said no more. He plainly meant that he would be prepared, as Prime Minister, to stand such a strike in order to break through on productivity—instead of giving ground at the last minute, in the usual way of negotiations.

It is this willingness to offend powerful interests that makes Heath a potential radical reformer of such interest. There are signs of this character in his background. At Oxford, he broke with the Conservative party to support an anti-Munich candidate in a 1938 by-election. His 1964 fight against retail price-fixing showed a similar disdain for party habit. The question is whether his rather wooden manner can communicate any fire to the voters.

If Heath and the Conservatives somehow upset the predictions and win this Thursday, they are going to do it on issues, not personality. And Heath has done the job of building a campaign on issues, as the outs should do.

There is really only one issue—the decaying British economy and what to do about it. The Conservative answer is completely Ted Heath's: ruthless competition. In his few months as leader, no one can deny, he has put his philosophical imprint heavily on a party filled with languid types who hardly look like the managerial revolution.

The Conservative platform, a punchy 4,500 words, read like a technocrat's manual. More important, it promised a head-on assault against the featherbedding, wildcat strikes and other trade-union malpractices that frustrate industrial life here. It was no softer on the incompetent managements that infest industry. Companies, it said, must pay a bigger share of their employes' social insurance costs, thus pressing managements to stop hoarding scarce labor and using it at half-pace. Government subsidies must be cut, and even tariffs reduced, to force competition. And, finally, Britain must have the cold bath of Common Market membership.

When Labor released its platform a few days later, the contrast could not have been greater. In 11,000 murky words the old war cries were sounded—renationalize steel, have the Government "plan" construction and industrial growth, subsidize existing nationalized industries if necessary. What would be done about restrictive practices by labor and management? The Prime Minister would hold a conference. The Common Market? Labor was ready to join—if the six countries of the community would meet all conditions, including abandonment of their vital agricultural pricing system.

The very room in which the press conference releasing the platform was held seemed symbolic—a Transport Workers' hall displaying nineteen-twentyish murals of semi-nude ladies holding models of the streetcars, trains and biplanes of that day. A young, modernist Labor candidate who was present at the press conference buried his head in his hands and said he would somehow manage to campaign on his own ideas about Europe and competition. Even the pro-Labor Guardian wrote an editorial the next day sarcastically criticizing the party manifesto.

The truth is that Harold Wilson is the tactical master of the Labor party but has by no means been able to modernize its expressed ideology. It is the only democratic Socialist party in Europe that still proclaims such quaint dogma. And it is tied to one of the most reactionary vested interests in the country, the trade-union movement.

What saves the Labor party from self-strangulation is the widespread belief that Harold Wilson in practice will pay little or no attention to the proclaimed dogmas. That belief has a basis. An authoritative account of the Prime Minister's plans a month after he took office in October, 1964, spoke of his "determination to go ahead and renationalize steel, to nationalize urban building land, to broaden social welfare." Except for some marginal welfare improvements, the Wilson Government has not yet even started a bill through Parliament to achieve one of those objectives.

The Wilson Government, in fact, has done rather little reforming. Mostly, it has just existed—staving off disaster to the pound, protecting its own parliamentary majority. Wilson has shrewdly appealed in the campaign for Labor to be given a real chance to govern, with a real majority. At the same time, he has played on the achievement of merely existing in difficult circumstances. His slogan is: "You know Labor Government works."

What may worry some voters is the possibility that Wilson with a majority of 50 or 150 may be a different animal from the one hemmed in by a majority of only three; perhaps he would then revert to militant Socialism. Conversely, there are doubts about the thoroughness of Heath's modernist revolution within the Conservative party; class-based suspicions remain of the over-whelming Tory old-boy element.

In the campaign, the most discouraging episode to genuine reformers of all parties has been Mr. Wilson's negative response to the French indication that Britain is now welcome in the Common Market. Mr. Wilson said he welcomed the idea of membership—but that "we must be free to go on buying food and raw materials, as we have for 100 years, in the cheapest [Commonwealth] markets." That condition could be described, mildly, as unrealistic. The reformers would say that the whole point of Britain's plight is that she must change the habits of 100 years. Fortunately, they have come not to place too much weight on what Mr. Wilson says in campaigns.

Whoever is elected, events will probably control the course of the Government more than the promises of the last month. The fate of the pound is truly at stake. The realist trying to make a choice Thursday, uninfluenced by emotion or tradition, would probably do best to pick the man he thinks is most likely to say "no" to the forces that are making Britain fat and lazy and selfish.

Suggested Reading

Mark Abrams and Richard Rose, *Must Labour Lose?*, Harmondsworth, Eng., Penguin Books, 1960 (paperback).

E. Eldon Barry, *Nationalization in Britain: The Historical Background*, Stanford, Calif., Stanford University Press, 1965.

Lord Beaverbrook, *The Decline and Fall of Lloyd George*, New York, Duell, Sloan and Pearce, 1963.

Nora Beloff, *The General Says No*, Harmondsworth, Eng., Penguin Books, 1963 (paperback).

Angus Calder, *The People's War: Britain, 1939–1945*, New York, Pantheon, 1969.

Colin Cross, *The Fascists in Britain*, New York, St. Martin's, 1963.

William Davis, *Three Years Hard Labour: The Road to Devaluation*, Boston, Houghton Mifflin, 1970.

Constantine Fitzgibbon, *The Blitz*, London, Macdonald, 1970.

Paul Foot, *The Politics of Harold Wilson*, Harmondsworth, Eng., Penguin Books, 1968 (paperback).

Martin Gilbert and Richard Gott, *The Appeasers*, Boston, Houghton Mifflin, 1963.

Roy F. Harrod, *The Life of John Maynard Keynes*, London, Macmillan, 1951 (St. Martin's paperback).

Harry Hopkins, *The New Look: A Social History of the Forties and Fifties in Britain*, Boston, Houghton Mifflin, 1964.

Alfred E. Kahn, *Great Britain in the World Economy*, New York, Columbia University Press, 1946.

Ben W. Lewis, *British Planning and Nationalization*, New York, Twentieth Century Fund, 1952.

Basil Liddell Hart, "The Military Strategist," in A. J. P. Taylor *et al.*, *Churchill: Four Faces and the Man*, London, Allen Lane: The Penguin Press, 1969.

Almont Lindsey, *Socialized Medicine in England and Wales: The National Health Service, 1948–1961*, Chapel Hill, University of North Carolina Press, 1962.

David Low, *Low's Autobiography*, New York, Simon and Schuster, 1957.

Richard Lyman, *The First Labour Government, 1924*, London, Chapman and Hall, 1957.

W. N. Medlicott, *British Foreign Policy Since Versailles, 1919–1963*, 2nd ed., New York, Barnes and Noble, 1968 (University paperback).

Drew Middleton, *The Sky Suspended: The Battle of Britain*, New York, McKay, 1960.

Nancy Mitford, ed., *Noblesse Oblige: An Enquiry into the Identifiable Characteristics of the English Aristocracy*, New York, Harper and Row, 1956 (Penguin paperback).

John F. Naylor, *Labour's International Policy: The Labour Party in the 1930's*, Boston, Houghton Mifflin, 1969.

Anthony Nutting, *No End of a Lesson: The Story of Suez*, New York, Clarkson Potter, 1967.

Henry Pelling, *Britain and the Second World War*, London, Fontana Library, 1970 (paperback).

John Raymond, ed., *The Baldwin Age*, Chester Springs, Pa., Dufour, 1961.

A. L. Rowse, *Appeasement: A Study in Political Decline, 1933–1939*, New York, Norton, 1961 (paperback).

Andrew Shonfield, *British Economic Policy Since the War*, Harmondsworth, Eng., Penguin Books, 1959 (paperback).

Michael Sissons and Philip French, eds., *Age of Austerity, 1945–1951*, Mystic, Conn., Lawrence Verry, 1963 (Penguin paperback).

Robert Skidelsky, *Politicians and the Slump: The Labour Government of 1929–1931*, New York, Humanities Press, 1967.

Hugh Thomas, *Suez,* New York, Harper and Row, 1967 (paperback).

W. Thornhill, *The Nationalized Industries: An Introduction,* London, Nelson, 1968.

Richard M. Titmuss, *Essays on the Welfare State,* 2nd ed., Boston, Beacon Press, 1969 (paperback).

Trevor Wilson, *The Downfall of the Liberal Party, 1914–1935,* Ithaca, Cornell University Press, 1967.

Index

A Note on the Editor

John F. Naylor was born in Newburgh, New York, and studied at Hamilton College and at Harvard University, where he was a Woodrow Wilson Fellow. Mr. Naylor is the author of *Labour's International Policy* and *The British Aristocracy and the Peerage Bill of 1719,* and is now Associate Professor of History at the State University of New York at Buffalo.